Catching Cornwall in Flight

or

THE BETTERMOST CLASS OF PEOPLE

K. C. Phillipps

CORNISH HILLSIDE PUBLICATIONS
ST. AUSTELL, CORNWALL

ISBN 0 9519419 4 1

Published by Cornish Hillside Publications
St. Austell, Cornwall

Typeset by Kestrel Data, Exeter
Printed in Great Britain by Short Run Press Ltd, Exeter

For Josephine Sackett

By the same author

Jane Austen's English
Westcountry Words and Ways
The Language of Thackeray
Language and Class in Victorian England
A Glossary of the Cornish Dialect

Forthcoming Publications

The Journals of Charles Lee
Roche Rhymes

Contents

Acknowledgements

For the illustrations in this book I am greatly indebted to the keepers of the Phillipps' 'archive' in Roche, Mrs A. Paynter and Mrs D. Hooper; and to the keepers of the more scattered Hawken photographs, Mrs J. Trethewey of Roche, Mrs C. Wood of Huddersfield and Mrs R. Snell of St. Austell. Extra photographs of Roche School in the thirties were supplied by that very faithful Rocher, Mrs Una Poad; by Miss Jenifer Harvey, daughter of the former schoolmaster, and by Mr Charles Thurlow, the publisher of this book. Mr Simon Parker of *The Western Morning News* was a great help with pre-publication publicity.

The originator of it all is the person to whom the book is dedicated: Miss Josephine Sackett, who prompted and encouraged for a long time. Mr Ted Gallacher of Nottingham kept warning me when I was growing too provincial. Dr John Rowe and his wife, Constance, having first warned me that writing an autobiography set in Roche would mean that I should have to buy a single ticket to Fiji, nevertheless gave me much encouragement and practical advice.

My wife masterminded the transition from an elderly to an electric typewriter, and retyped the whole script, to the relief of the publisher, who saw the original! She also ensured that the tone of the work was less dyspeptic.

Last but by no means least I should like to thank my former colleague at Leicester, Emeritus Professor Jack Simmons, for his generous and perceptive foreword.

SCHOOL HOUSE, MOUNT
1994

Foreword

I was honoured by Ken Phillipps's request that I should write a brief preface to this book. When he made it to me, I said I felt it would be more suitably introduced by someone who was Cornish. But he wanted a note about it from an external point of view and he thought of me because we were for a long time colleagues and friends far away, in the University of Leicester. His book treats his life from within – within himself and his family, within Cornwall. I offer an outsider's view of what he has to tell us.

Many people have set themselves to record the stories of their own lives, in autobiographies. Some of these books concentrate attention almost entirely on the writer's own life and thoughts. Others have been at pains to set their lives in the context of their families and the society in which they grew up. This book is one of the second kind.

It is an autobiography only in part. The writer is at the centre of it, in touch with us continuously, relating from his personal knowledge, explaining and commenting on what he has remembered and found out, speaking directly of his likes and dislikes. He sees the writing of an autobiography as "chiefly an indulgence in egotism". But it can be much more than that, and it is so here. For whilst he is present and addressing his readers all the time, the heart of what he is writing about is not himself alone. His subject is expressed in the phrase he has chosen for his sub-title; interpreted, as he explains at the outset, in a moral sense as meaning "the best people I knew in mid-Cornwall, from 1935 to 1950".

His story begins at Roche, a place so curious physically that once seen it can never be forgotten, with the medieval chapel perched up on its steep, gaunt rock. We learn here that it is "the most plebeian village in Cornwall"; it has no large house that ever set any example, good or bad. This is emphatically a book about mid-Cornwall; the sea enters into it very little. Visitors from England, driving down into the country along the A38, may perhaps (if they use their eyes) be just conscious of the amplitude of Bodmin Moor as they cross it, but they still hasten on to the coast. How often I have heard people say that the cliffs and beaches of Cornwall are fine, but there is nothing worth looking at inland. This book reveals a little of what they have missed.

One thing that marks it off from nearly all other autobiographies is the extent to which it is an account of a life illuminated and played upon by a dialect. A number of the best twentieth-century autobiographies (referred to here with appreciation), relating to Cornwall and to other parts of England, have made use of dialect words and phrases, enriching and invigorating their writers' own minds. Ken Phillipps has listened to this speech with close attention, as can be seen from his admirable *Glossary of the Cornish Dialect*, published last year. But he has also been a student and teacher of the English language, so he is skilful in showing us the relationship between language and dialect, and in deciding what can be most fitly expressed by means of one rather than the other.

He introduces us first to his family, in particular to his notable father and grandfather and to a striking group of aunts. (Who will write about the aunt for us, as she has appeared in English literature from Jane Austen to our own time?) This is linked to the general shop they kept, not only to the ways in which it was stocked and run but also to shopping itself, as an art and craft: the triumphant pouncing on bargains, the comparison of prices from one shop to another, always to somebody's discredit.

And then, treated on its own: the Chapel. Methodism is presented to us here in a livelier and more congenial way than in most of the historical works devoted to it. The conversation centred on the chapels, the attitudes of mind they formed, the religious and social life they have moulded and framed, are shown to us in a clear, straightforward way that anyone can understand. This account has put me in mind of *Mrs Beer's House*, from Devon, the book in which Patricia Beer gave me and a good many other people a much more intelligible and sympathetic view of the Plymouth Brethren than any that had been offered before. But with this vital difference: that the Brethren were a minute, tightly- knit, secluded sect, whereas Methodism and all its variations built up and retained down to the time that is treated of here a power and a strong influence of its own throughout Cornwall.

This book catches time on the wing, with its frequent comparisons and contrasts between the Cornwall of fifty years ago and the Cornwall of today. A higher and higher proportion of the people who are living in the county but were not born there appears in each successive census. And then there is the pervasive, insidious influence of radio and television, with all the other devices working on passive minds. "It will be a sad day" (p. 47) "when humour arises from second-hand sources, from sitcom and videoed comedy, and not from real-life situations".

I agree with that remark, and yet I don't altogether accept the view it conveys of the present and future. I first came to Cornwall just at the beginning of the time to which this book relates, and I have been back to it, to see much-valued friends there, ever since. I still feel that, among the forty historic English counties, this is the one that, in spite of all the flattening, equalising tendencies of modern life, remains the most distinct: in landscape (though beware of motorways, or there will be an M599 from Indian Queens to Newquay), in social relations and, so far as I can catch it, in speech. I don't believe that all this is going; and a book like this one, speaking out plainly, helps to indicate some of the things that are most worth trouble to keep and protect.

J. S.

Introduction

A Roche man on a coach trip: Handsome
houses here, sure 'nough
His wife: Truro, see! bettermost class of people.

Writing an autobiography is chiefly an indulgence in egotism; but
I did have a few other motives as well. I wanted to record a little
of what Daphne du Maurier entitles 'Vanishing Cornwall': the
dialect, the attitudes and outlook, and the cooking. These things
amounted to a provincial culture – some would say a national one;
though an entity does not prove to be a Cornish nation, it seems
to me, if one has to go to Twickenham, or Tottenham, or
somewhere else to assert this.

I am interested chiefly in inland Cornwall; the Cornwall that
fifty years ago was concerned with Methodism and teetotalism to
a considerable extent, and not, as we might assume from Daphne
du Maurier's novels, with 'drunken sailors'. I was given a lively
reminder of this fact by our family solicitor who presented me with
a Minute Book of the former Roche Temperance Hall (the minutes
mostly kept by my father and grandfather), and including some
trenchant criticism of the (licensed) Rock Hotel (now the Rock
Inn). There were of course divergent elements; but the consensus
in the china clay villages was for sobriety, thrift and honest dealing.
Obviously, inland Cornwall extended over a wider area, and was
more populous than seaboard Cornwall.

In this respect I should like to think that my book shuns pre-
vious littoral stereotypes. I should like to forget the labyrinthine
smugglers' tunnels, as endless, seemingly, as the tunnels of 'wants'
(moles), that lead from every smugglers' cave to the cellars of
every squire's house within a radius of six miles. I should like to
ignore the composers who write piano concertos for lady pianists,

beautiful but demented, to play on windswept Cornish cliffs. At least away from the coast we keep our feet on the ground! And inland Cornwall is liveable and lively all the year round; not merely when there is an 'r' in the month. I still chuckle at the memory of being in the wide doorway of a bookshop in one of our coastal towns, in a deluge of rain and with hordes of visitors milling around. The water was flowing in at the toes of their sandals and out at the heels. All of a sudden a backwoods voice, more used perhaps to calling 'Oke! Oke! Oke!' to bring the cows in, cried out: "I said to mawther, I said 'Damn th' old visitors; they'm always under your feet!' " I fear that this is in no sense a visitors' book.

There have been at least two outstanding autobiographies from Cornwall this century. One is A. L. Rowse's *A Cornish Childhood*, the other is Anne Treneer's *School House in the Wind*. Both have the same limitation, from the point of view of representing Cornish life: neither author was brought up a Methodist. One short book that does present this viewpoint is *Cornish Youth*, by Tom Tremewan, of Perranporth. Fifty years ago, at the time of this present autobiography, Methodism was easily the majority religion. I make no apology for dwelling on the subject.

In the Cornish dialect the phrase of my sub-title means the upper middle classes, probably; but I should like to extend this meaning from a sociolinguistic to a moral one: 'the best people I knew in mid-Cornwall, from 1935 to 1950'.

I have been told that you are not an established writer until you have received your first hate mail, as I did recently. Like most hate mail this was unsigned. There were two counts in the indictment: (1) I was probably not Cornish; (2) I was 'letting down my own people'. I hope the second chapter will answer the first objection. Phillipps, it is true, does not sound a very Cornish name; it would be better if I were called Polkinghorne perhaps, or Penaluna. But I cannot do much about that. All I would claim, and it is a statement not a boast, is that to the best of my knowledge and belief I do not have a drop of Anglo- Saxon blood in my veins. My wife, Pat, finds that this concentration of the Celtic accounts for some awkwardness in my temperament: 'If they'd put you through the blender you would have been blander', she says.

As to 'letting down my own people', I don't think many inhabitants of Roche (and they are the people who matter most to me) would think I had let anybody down. My father used to say that he didn't really like anyone he couldn't tease a bit; and this is a traditional pastime of Cornish writers over the past hundred years – to poke kindly fun, to pull the collective leg of

Cornwall, but in such a way that affection still shows through. I am thinking of Quiller Couch, Charles Lee, Claude Berry, A. L. Rowse, Anne Treneer, Charles Causley and so on.

But the really disquieting thing is whether there will soon be anything specifically Cornish to tease people about. The question is not whether we shall be 'ballyragged' (annoyed), but whether we shall be forgotten. The threat is not persecution but oblivion.

It was suggested to me that since the non-native population of Cornwall is now greater than the native, we Cornish should consider ourselves an élite. The trouble is, I feel sure that such illusory ideas may well have been current in 838, before the battle of Hingston Down, where Ecgbert of Wessex defeated the Cornish finally; or so it is supposed. However, in one sense this battle was never finished. As one reads the local press or listens to Radio Cornwall, skirmishes between Celtic and non-Celtic forces appear to continue. In any case, there is no room for complacency.

The answer may well be to follow the example of the philosopher, William James, who recommended doing something every so often for no other reason than that you do not particularly want to do it. So one trains one's character to duty. In much the same way we Cornish ought to do things for no other reason than that they are Cornish; because, as was explained to me long ago (and I still acknowledge the truth of it) if we cease to be Cornish we shall not be anything very much at all.

One of the surest ways for regional characteristics to assert themselves is through regional speech. Yet until I began writing about our dialect in *The Western Morning News* in 1970, virtually nothing had been published on the subject since the Courtney Couch Glossary of 1880; apart, that is, from *The Leeds Dialect Survey* of the nineteen-sixties, which is inaccessible except to those with a knowledge of the International Phonetics Alphabet.

With characteristic Phillipps diffidence, having written the article I put it away. 'Twas all very well writing for learned journals; nobody read those. But an article for *The Western Morning News* could be read more widely – perhaps in Roche! More hardened in wickedness, I eventually wrote sixty articles for my favourite newspaper; and forty elsewhere. I collected a large box full of correspondence, some of which continues; for there is still a real and increasingly urgent interest in the dialect of Cornwall.

Dialect does not die out 'all to once' of course; it is more like the former villages and towns on the East Anglian coast, like Dunwich, for example, that gradually are eroded and disappear into the sea.

Pride, or to give it a less outspoken name, refinement, is perhaps the biggest enemy. There is no doubt that the Cornish dialect, like most of the dialects of Britain, is in the 'refiner's fire'. I particularly single out the refined 'mummy' as a major eroding influence. Often I have been told, 'Mummy wouldn't let us speak in dialect'.

Mummy ought to be asked two questions: first, what is to become of her children's 'Cornishry', to adopt a recent term, if they are to anticipate in their speech a forthcoming state of affairs when Cornwall is to be an outer suburb of London? The second question to ask is why does mummy underrate her children's intelligence? I sometimes take part in a conversation with a young man from East Cornwall, and we speak in broadish dialect: for the sake of variety he will sometimes break off, and being a live wire he will talk 'absolutely marvellously' so to speak, in a passable imitation of Prince Charles. Nearly all young people can be bi-lingual in this way.

The term autobiography with which I began this Introduction, proves to be not entirely accurate, as Professor Simmons sees. For one thing I realised somewhat ruefully that the relatives I describe were at least as interesting as I was. Accordingly on the whole, except for an occasional 'overspill' I have confined my own life-story to the middle chapters.

An additional motive was to put the village of Roche on the map, and to remind Rochers of our status as natives of one of the most historically interesting places in the West Country. This is in despite of hordes of people from 'upward where times is brisk', as the dialect phrase goes, who are over-populating the place. Roche is beginning to take on the appearance of a straggling 'townlet', there being no adequate centre to the village to serve these extra people; though amenities are partly provided to the extent that now the public lavatories are probably the only secular public building not furnished with a bar! When I think of the years during which my father struggled to keep a bar out of the Victory Hall!

Personally I have learnt not to disregard Roche opinions, having found them a guide and a corrective over the years. For instance, when I was nearly tempted into buying an ill-fitting suit, I remembered a Roche remark about an unfortunate new hat: "Whoever sold Auntie Beat that hat ought to be summonsed." '

There has always been a saving commonsense in the village. I once told my mother that in Leicester we had been invited to midday Sunday drinks: "Well, yes, Kenneth" she said, "but I should think 'twould spoil your appetite for Sunday dinner." It did, of course. My imaginings about all the juggling with money represented by over-hyped television advertising about insurance, are expressed in a phrase of fifty years ago. A rather simple Roche youth, 'put in with the bread and took out with the cake' as we say, managed to land himself a job in a St. Austell shop. "So", said my former friend Bryn Lean "if we want a shillingsworth of half-crowns, that is where we'll have to go." I suspect that quite a lot of financial jiggery-pokery can be summed up in the phrase 'a shillingsworth of half-crowns'.

I must beware of giving too much rein to nostalgia. It is good to remember a Mr Olver from Mevagissey who came down Trezaise Road on a motor-bike with a sidecar full of fish, calling out "Whiting and pilchards!" but it is still better to boast, as my sister did recently, "We got a fishmonger in Roche now!"

Of the writing of books on Cornwall, as of books generally, there is no end. Rather too prevalent perhaps is what I call the 'studies-in-St. Ives-chimney-pots' variety. In such a book the imagination is not deeply engaged. But at least such treatises avoid the inauthentic; and in any event these are not usually as badly written as what I call the 'simply lashings' type of Cornish book. This will have been written by an upper middle- class holiday-maker from the Home Counties: 'So we had a scrumptious tea with oodles of cake covered with simply lashings of cream.' I am sure we have never talked like that. A dark brown pottery creambowl in Devon earthenware which I remember from my childhood, and which bore the legend 'Go aisy with the crame now', corresponds more with reality.

As I put the finishing touches to this book, in a cold but still promising spring in Mount, I am aware of the need to keep in touch with all that is happening in the county. It will not do to say as the hypochondriac Mr Woodhouse says in Jane Austen's *Emma*, "I live out of the world and I am often astonished by what I hear." The curious thing is that though Mount is fairly remote, I do learn a great deal of what goes on. Indeed I sometimes flatter myself with one of my favourite quotations: "If a man can write a better book, preach a better sermon, or make a better mousetrap than his neighbour, though he build his house in the woods the world will make a beaten path to his door." That was the American sage, Ralph Waldo Emerson. I hope the reader is impressed; but I cannot tell a lie. I did not read this great thought in any book; I read it on a mousetrap that we sold in our shop. It was called the Better Mousetrap; better because it had a handle so you couldn't trap your fingers.

But it cost sixpence.

In my memory, I seem to hear voices murmuring as they take their purchase down Roche Hill from the shop. "Sixpence! My gar, that's some dear for a mousetrap. Cheap in half the money! I used to think they party didn't overcharge; but they'm overcharging now, sure, 'nough. Sixpence for a mousetrap! I never heared tell of such a thing."

Chapter 1

The Rock

Look unto the rock whence ye are hewn

The first thing that everyone learns about the village of Roche is the existence of the Rock. The early charters are full of Latin and French variants of the name of the most important family in the district in the time of Richard I – the de Rupes or the de la Roches and earlier still is the name of the manor farm, Tregarrick from the Cornish 'carek', a rocky mass or a huge rock.

The next thing to notice is the sheer improbability of it all. Thus the Rock struck Sir Nicholas Pevsner, in the Cornwall volume of 'The Buildings of England' as 'improbable as if it were some 19th century Victorian play of fantasy in a public park . . . a phenomenon as impressive now in industrial surroundings as it must have been in the rural solitude of the Middle Ages.'

As the seasons change also, the Rock is full of surprises. In snowy weather a villager may exclaim, 'The Rock do look purdy today' and indeed it does look like a gigantic piece of confectionery under its icing of snow. It looks good too, as I have seen it, on windy and cloudy moonlit nights, with rays of the moon dappling the old stones with alternate light and shade.

But perhaps more remarkable than the geology of the Rock is its history; for in 1409 in this high place, and 50 feet above ground, a chapel was built and dedicated to St. Michael. The questions one wants to ask are endless. How many limbs, and how many necks were broken before the East Window ('big window' we used to call it) was fixed in place? What work it must have needed to scoop out the hermit's cell below! How did they raise these massive granite blocks 'as big as chests of drawers' into position? To use a dialect word, what 'louster' (hard labour) it must all have been! This might have been one of those bursts or blasts of religious

1

fervour of which we caught a few late random gusts in Roche when I was a boy.

For some time, at the beginning of the 15th century, it must have been a novelty – 'a new vang' – to climb up on to the Rock (no convenient ladders then, of course) to attend a service. Gradually the chapel was disused, except that for a time, according to a widespread legend, it was the home of a hermit, who was also a leper. He was waited on ('tended to inches' would be the dialect phrase) by his daughter, Gunnett or Gundred. She fetched him water for drinking and washing. There was supposed to be a well near the Rock which rose and fell with the tide but I don't suppose anyone really believed that. More probably, Gunnett may have gone for water a mile to the south, to Reeshill, where the youthful River Fal skips along on the way to the Goss Moor. She would probably not have gone so near Hensbarrow as the headspring of the Fal at Pentevale.

But I think, with her father's leprosy in mind, she would have been content with nothing less than water from Roche's Holy Well. It is a 'brave little step', a mile or so, from the Rock. To make such a journey now Gunnett would have had to cross the A30, and there is no greater contrast in Roche today than that between the rumpus of the A30 and the untroubled little pool, with its medieval superstructure, in its little dell.

The hermit and his daughter are both long dead, and the chapel on the Rock has been roofless for more than 300 years. What remains is the romantic frame of a church surviving in industrial surroundings. For Roche is now an 'island settlement' encircled by heaps of 'micaceous' and other waste material tipped by the china clay industry. The legends have mostly been forgotten. Few Roche people, I imagine, now lie awake on stormy nights wondering if the mid-Cornwall giant, Tregeagle,[1] had got his head stuck in 'big window'. So far as I know, nobody even goes 'out Rock' for picnics and to play 'mopp and hideaway' among the boulders, as we did in the 'holidays at home' period during the war.

---

1 Perhaps the most interesting of all the comparisons that occur in the Cornish dialect is that used when a roaring wind, or the loud crying of a child, is said to be 'like Tregeagle'. Tregeagle, who flourished in the Cromwellian period, was an unjust and cruel bailiff for the lords of Lanhydrock, and he has had grafted on to him several legends perhaps formerly attributed to the devil. Tregeagle himself is driven by devils and is condemned for ever to drain Dozmary Pool, in the bleakest part of Bodmin Moor, with a leaky limpet shell.

In Ward Lock's guide to the Newquay area, published in the nineteen-twenties, the Holy Well is described as being visited by the 'peasantry', who invoke the blessing of the Saint, preferably before sunrise on Holy Thursday. Not being nice observers of church festivals, and not much liking to rise early, we Methodist peasantry used to visit the Holy Well on summer rambles, taking with us our pins to throw into the water. One part of the ceremony we all observed: the pins must be bent. The Dexters in their *Cornish Crosses* connect this twisting of the metal with curved carvings on the oldest and most primitive-shaped cross in Roche churchyard.

Very occasionally, over the decades, the Rock has hit the headlines – as with 'Roche's Big Bang' some forty-odd years ago in the *Cornish Guardian*. The occasion was a firework display to give a somewhat belated finality to the end of the Second World War. There was in Roche, of course, only one place for such a display to occur – from the top of the Rock. One of the more timid members of the fireworks' committee told the others that he would look after the unused fireworks in the hermit's cell, while they let them off one by one from the top. My father, from his stock as an ironmonger, had selected Cornish shovel hilts as improvised 'launching pads' for the rockets.

The outcome might have been predictable; one or two sparks from the first rockets set off the rest. Those of us who remained at ground level were astonished to hear, after the first few fireworks, a thunderous series of explosions, as if Tregeagle himself were suffering from a severe bout of indigestion. The committee man in the lower chamber found himself in a ball of fire and 'skiddered' down the ladder at top speed. It was left to a local wit, my uncle Will, to add the last word: "I put down," he said, "there was Russian reconnaissance planes taking photographs of they shovel hilts".

Anyway, there it stands: 'Despite the storms I stand' was a motto we learnt about the Rock at Roche school. If it was a few miles nearer the coast there would be dainty teas, turnstiles and 50p extra to go into the hermit's cell; but Roche was never dainty. As it is, entrance is entirely free, by kind permission, a rusty notice explains, of Lord Falmouth. Yet from time to time, when, for example, geology students chip off a bit of schorl, I for one find it annoying. For deep down every Roche person born and bred thinks of the Rock as his heritage.

In the Penguin guide to Cornwall (1947), Roche is described as 'an oasis of interest in a dreary district'. The surrounding china clay industry, however prosperous it has been, has had a pretty disastrous effect, scenically, on the neighbourhood. Probably most visitors do not linger long today, any more than the Elizabethan topographer Richard Carew, of Antony, did:

'After we have quitted Restormel, Roche becomes our next place of sojourn; though hardly inviting with promise of any better entertainment than the name carieth written in his forehead, to wit, a huge high and steep rock seated in a plain, girded on either side with . . . two substitutes. From hence ascending easily the space of a mile, you shall have won the top of the Cornish archbeacon, Hainborough . . . If the weather's darkness bound not your eyesight, within his ordinary extent you shall therein plainly discern, to the Eastward, a great part of Devon, to the West very near the Land's End, to the North and South, the ocean and sundry islands scattered therein.'

I thought of these remarks of Carew when, with a friend, I walked over Hensbarrow (as we now call it) recently. Suddenly half hidden by china clay workings and surrounded by whitened and polluted turf, there appeared before us the barrow and beacon that Carew knew and which more recently has been the traditional site of midsummer bonfires. Hensbarrow is also, or was, the best place I know for whortleberries in July, or 'hurts', as we call them. It is the occupation of a more patient age to pick these little berries; but the flavour is rewarding. I wonder also, as the village becomes urbanised, what will happen to the spectacular moorland black-berries that follow in September. Anne Treneer pays tribute in her *Cornish Years*: she speaks of 'spending summers at Roche, and tasting the great juicy blackberries that grow on the moors there'; I suppose such fruit will hereafter be picked in Poland, imported and sold in supermarkets here.

The direction from the village which is freest from pollution is the north-east, to places like Tremodret (the only Cornish place-name to incorporate the name of Modred, villain of Arthurian legend), and also Highertown and Criggan, all three important places for our family. But even here, the march of suburbanisation proceeds with concrete boots. I can imagine with what enthusiasm the civic authorities will greet these 'improvements'; and I know precisely the obscenities which Roche people, who have never shied away from a four-letter word, will apply.

The aforementioned road to Tremodret is crossed by a white-railed bridge, bearing the little trains that ply between Newquay on the north coast and Par on the south; more immediately, between the two stations of Roche and Bugle.

4

It must be obvious that I am fighting shy of describing the natural scenery of the village; one good reason for this is that, apart from the Rock, there is not much spectacular to see. Another reason is that I bear in mind a remark of Jane Austen's which also applies to myself: 'My preference for men and women always inclines me to attend more to the company than the sight'. I well remember father telling me off when we were in a train going to Plymouth through the splendid Glynn Valley, because I spent the time speculating on a torrid flirtation that was going on in the same carriage.

Chapter 2

Ancestors

*When genealogy comes in at the door, truth flies out of the
window*

When anyone asks me, "Have the Phillippses always lived in the
village of Roche?" I answer with some pride, "I don't know;
because the parish records go back only to the fifteen nineties;
but we were here then". It took my New Zealand cousins, from
Dunedin, clutching their more fragmentary family trees and cling-
ing to the double 'p' of their surname, to alert me to how
long-established we had been in the parish. Most prominent of the
visitors was cousin Ron Phillipps, a former director of education
in Otago province; later, but equally welcome, was cousin Donald,
a Methodist minister and formerly President of the New Zealand
Methodist Conference. Ron went back to his homeland with a
family tree and a largely bogus coat of arms. Donald travelled
home with some Wisdens he had collected – he regaled us all with
tales of cricketers of yore whom we should undoubtedly see playing
again all the time in heaven; thus confirming my suspicion that
heaven might be a bit dull.

Most of the early Phillippses, of course, are names only. It is not
until my great-great-great grandfather, the long-lived William
(1766–1851) that a personality emerges. Among other things, he
carved his own tombstone and kept it in a cupboard in his house
at Higher Trerank, near Roche church. The headstone can still be
seen (vandals permitting) in the churchyard. William's son Thomas
(1807–62) followed the Phillipps pattern of a quieter offspring in
the generation following a flamboyant one. It is said that on his
death-bed Thomas sent his son, Job, to get a fill of pipe-tobacco,
and that Job was extremely reluctant, because he hated the smell
of it. Incidentally, Job would later not allow a man to smoke in
his blacksmith's shop, where the air was probably none too pure

in any case. Passive smoking in the eighteen seventies! There is nothing new under the sun. These things are an allegory; because with my great-grandfather, Job, the Phillippses became immersed in Methodism. Job did not take long to become a local preacher, a school governor and builder of a solid Victorian house that still stands. He was also, I think, the first to take up the family calling of blacksmith, where before tin-mining and 'the millerin' had been traditional.

The original home, the *Urheimat* of the Phillipps family, was not Higher Trerank but Rosemellin, between Roche and what is now Bugle. In Maclean's *Parochial and Family History of the Deanery of Trigg Minor* (p. 285) one William Phillipps was seen to be established in Rosemellin, with several grown-up children, long before his death in 1757. Clearly this is another William Phillipps, living in a more prestigious place. The relationship between the descendants of the Rosemellin William and the various Phillipps names that occur in Roche parish records, is not easy to trace. If there had not been two drastic restorations of the parish church in the last century, some of these Rosemellin Phillippses, obviously of 'the bettermost class of people', as they still say in the South-West, might well have had memorial tablets or monuments in Roche church, if not in Lanivet. William of Rosemellin begat Nicholas, who begat another William. Nicholas was rector, and the second William rector and patron, of the neighbouring parish of Lanivet, said to be the midmost village in Cornwall, and certainly the place where Thomas Hardy did some of his courting. Maclean's *Trigg Minor* details permission to use Phillipps along with Flamank as, presumably, a double-barrelled name, Phillipps-Flamank. But I do not for one moment think that this applied to all mid-Cornwall Phillippses, and neither did the coat of arms recommended by Maclean, which my New Zealand cousin took home with such pride, viz. two lions rampant (also on the crest) and the motto *Virtus ad astra*, courage to the stars.

But this is not all. Of all the local preachers, of varied ability, who held forth at Trezaise Bible Christian chapel, one of the most interesting was H. M. Creswell Payne, whose *The Story of the Parish of Roche* (a much better book than its catchpenny title would suggest) appeared just after the last war. In his preaching Creswell Payne brought local history to life, describing, for instance, the three rivers that start in the parish: the Fal, that ends in Falmouth, the Allen, a tributary of the Camel, whose estuary is at Padstow, and the little river that flows through Luxulyan valley to Par. Then, seeing me in a pew, I remember he started up with the legend of the treasure of the Phillipps family. I quote from Creswell Payne's book:

'The sister of Mr John Keen, named by Hals[1] . . . married a Phillipps of Rosemellin, and carried her brother's wealth into that family . . . Of the Phillipps family two were rectors of the adjoining parish of Lanivet; there is a tradition that during the Civil War the family plate was buried in one of the brakes at Rosemellin, and never afterwards recovered.'

With a friend, and a metal detector, I went over the downs of Rosemellin (admittedly now much reduced by enclosure) and we found a marmalade top and a metal milk-churn label! I cannot pretend that I was surprised. The whole of this legend of lost treasure has the mark of something brewed after many years in the long-established Rock Hotel (once graciously so-called, though the earlier and current formula 'Rock Inn, Roll Out' is perhaps more appropriate). Though ever since I have known them the Phillippses have been non-drinkers, in former days drinking and boasting would have gone together.

Job (or Job Josias, to give him his full name) was the first ancestor of whom I heard by word of mouth. I must have been about seven when an eighty-year-old Mrs Rowse,[2] our neighbour in Trezaise Road, told me about his influence at Trezaise Chapel: "When your great-grandfather and his brother-in-law, Daniel Trethewey, walked into Trezaise Sunday School, you could hear a pin drop". She also told me that, with her friends, 'we maidens' (pronounced *med'ns*) she fell into the habit of arriving at Sunday morning chapel late. This was so that the young men, who

---

[1] Antiquary, who wrote rather fragmentary histories of Cornwall. Died in neighbouring St. Wenn, c. 1737.

[2] Mrs Rowse had a nephew, named Archie. Sixty years ago, about the time when I had just started at Roche school, he used to come to see his aunt in a little sports car, with his then girl friend Hilda.

Mrs Hilda Rowse! No name has better associations with our dialect. Enviably, she used to broadcast quite often on the Home Service (now diluted to Radio 4), using the late Ralph Wightman, for comic purposes, as a sort of human Wailing Wall: "I tell 'ee, Mr Wightman, 'tis some job, all these here forms we got to fill in. Father do get properly mazed 'bout it". I shall always remember her description of a Cornish woman who is ready to go out for the evening: 'all tiched up with her earrings'. That, as the young say nowadays, is 'brilliant'.

traditionally sat in the back pews (I can just remember this) would admire the maidens as they came in, looking at their finery, and perhaps their ankles! My great-grandfather noticed all this, and next Sunday he was in the porch, waiting for latecomers.

It had all happened sixty years before (this was the nineteen-thirties, and Job had died in 1889) but Mrs Rowse never forgot that talking-to: "After he had finished with we maidens, we never come late to chapel no more".

I do not think there can have been many in Cornwall at the time who enjoyed the role of disciplinarian more keenly. This can also be seen in a book by Charles T. Trevail, *The Life and Reminiscences of C.T.T., Luxulyan, Cornwall* (1926) C.T.T., as he generally called himself, was an enthusiastic (if perhaps a little naive) Methodist who 'got on' as they say, by not missing a trick.[1] He built first sheds, then dwelling-houses, then roads, becoming also a parish councillor, a member of the Rural District Council and eventually a Justice of the Peace. This was perhaps the climax of his career; but of course for many years before this he had been a local preacher. Indeed as a young man he had been tempted to join the Church of England by Bishop Benson (later Archbishop Benson), the first bishop of the new see of Truro. At a meeting in Truro 'Bishop Benson took me by the arm,' says C.T.T.

But the poor man was in the grip of more powerful forces than he knew. He had forgotten that the county town was still Bodmin. He had also forgotten the quarterly meeting and the local preachers' meeting to be held there; and a great day of reckoning it proved to be. 'It was at Bodmin,' C.T.T. tells us, 'that I was asked to appear before the committee, composed mainly of hard disciplinarians. Mr Job J. Phillipps was first spokesman'.

Oh yes, I dare say that Job J. Phillipps 'properly enjoyed hisself' that day long ago 'in to Bodmin'. I don't doubt (to use a dialect expression of uncertain origin, but undoubted impact) . . . I don't doubt he 'giv'd 'un bel tink'.

---

[1] C.T.T. was born in 1854; it is almost incredible to relate that his daughter-in-law died recently (1994) in Fowey, aged 108. Clearly my great-grandfather and C.T.T. were destined not to get on. When C.T.T. made a speech some time later, Job, the next speaker, described him as 'willing but not able' Nevertheless, C.T.T. did visit at Higher Trerank in grandma's day when they 'had the preacher for dinner', My father always said that Job's achievements in forty-seven years offset his arrogance.

He reminded me (C.T.T. tells us) of the history of the treatment the Nonconformist had received at the hands of the Anglican Church – how they spoke of the Nonconformist as illegitimate and without authority – of the laws that were passed at the instigation of the church to prohibit the Nonconformist from preaching. He said, 'You are going to help the enemy'.

I can just imagine how these words would thunder across the meeting, over to poor C.T.T. 'looking wisht', as we say. But however much my great-grandfather strutted in Methodist circles, elsewhere he might be reckoned among the small fry. Compared to, say, Viscount Boscawen, Lord Falmouth, for example, he did not rate very high. In 1888–9, the sixth Lord Falmouth ordered the building of a substantial farm house at Trerank Farm, Roche, and gave instructions to the builder, a man named Kaylor, to get this house built. But for some reason (and presumably contrary to Kaylor's wishes) a lot of the carpenter's work was subcontracted to Job's brother-in-law, Daniel Trethewey. Kaylor, vexed with this local contract, kept protesting that the wood was unseasoned: " 'Tis damp wood; I can smill it" (these are the words my grandfather repeated to me). There was full use of dialect 'back in they days'. I can just hear the accents as the news would be related: 'Well, see, it got on Daniel Trethewey's nerves so much that he was took bad and went back home up Trezaise, and went to bed'. A few days later he was dead, officially of typhoid fever.

There is in the Methodist Archive (formerly in the City Road, London but now in Manchester) a periodical called *The Bible Christian Magazine*. As I looked up the appropriate date (1889) I found, rather to my surprise, that my eyes filled with tears. This was the entry:

Daniel Trethewey, on the 8th April, and J. J. Phillipps on the 15th, both of Roche, Bodmin circuit; an unexpected and an almost irreparable loss.

For Job, my great-grandfather, had died too. He could bluster at a meeting; but this blow was too much for him. Between April 8th and April 15th Job had decided not to live.

As a young man who married into the Phillipps family is said to have commented: 'The trouble with the Phillippses is they'm all hang-ups'.

In that year (1889) there were no Easter celebrations at Trezaise chapel.

But what was to be done? Job was forty-seven when he died. Everything depended on his eldest son, the twenty-three-year old

Thomas Trethewey, named for his mother, Charlotte Trethewey. There had been four children by Charlotte, and then Job had been made a widower. He did something most unusual in Roche – he negotiated for a wife from South Wales, and so married Henrietta Townsend. Before he died Job fathered several more children, who came to live in the adjoining house that he had built. Their house may have been better than the seventeenth-century cottage, now burnt down, where the Trethewey Phillipps lived; but the Townsend Phillipps came to be despised by their step-relations for their relatively limited intelligence. This, I fear, is a great tendency in our family – to be bigotty. Bigottiness is a mixture of three parts conceit and one part diffidence, not to say cowardice. For good measure the Tretheweys also, of whom there were many in Roche, have always been known as a bigotty family.[1] My father used to say that his sister, at the age of about eight, used to taunt her Townsend relations: "What do you mean – your wheelabala? 'Tis our wheelabala. But in any case, it is called a wheelbarrow, not a wheelabala!". This combination of high IQ and sharp tongue has so far, to the age of eighty-six, served Auntie Alice well. As for the Townsend relations, many remain in mid-Cornwall, but some have gone to Newfoundland, whence some of them visited granda, I remember, just before the war.

Granda Phillipps, as I always called him, is, if anybody is, the hero of this book. He was what is called in Cornwall a 'little small man.[2] Once, when I was studying in London, I visited Madame

---

[1] The Trethewey influence remained strong. Granda was Thomas Trethewey Phillipps, father was Charles Trethewey Phillipps. Mrs Rowse, our neighbour, used to say that I should have been called Kenneth Trethewey Phillipps. By this time it could have been a double-barrelled name. What an appalling thought!

My Christian name of Kenneth is a Trezaise name. There were two Kenneth Tretheweys; and no true Trezaise person ever called me Ken. It was interesting to note that when I spent two years in Edinburgh the abbreviated form was not used there either, for the name of course is originally Scottish.

[2] Father contended that it was marrying a Trethewey that made the descendants of Job 'such short-asses'. Job had been over six feet tall; I well remember the high hatpeg above the door that gave entry to the living room at Higher Trerank. Job had built the house and had had the peg fixed. None of the later Phillipses could reach it with ease.

Tussaud's. I was suddenly struck by the resemblance between my grandfather and another 'little small' man from the Westcountry. 'Good little Thomas Hardy', said Henry James. My grandfather was a much lesser figure, of course, with no claim to fame; but you could say 'Good little Tom Phillipps'. Soon it began to emerge that he was on top of the business. Not so pompous as his father, nor so disorganised as his son was to be, he saw what needed to be done and did it. It cannot have been an advantage to him to have a somewhat aristocratic loftiness in regard to trade. Auntie Kathleen, his eldest daughter, talked of 'tradesmen cheating the public', and I suspect the phrase may have come from him. My mother used to say that when he had an account to deliver for work done (and no doubt scrupulously done), he would walk round the customer three times before handing the bill over. New Year's Day (traditionally a holiday for blacksmiths) was devoted to accounts, and apparently you could cut the atmosphere with a knife. This was because granda wanted to charge too little, and grandma wanted a bit more housekeeping.

But it was in this matter of courtship that granda did well for himself. He would have gone courting in the moorland hamlet of Criggan, between Tremodret and Bilberry, on the far outskirts of Roche parish. There used to be a photograph of him, climbing up a small tree, which somehow suggests a vigorous manhood. At Criggan lived the Knight family – two boys, Mike and Charlie, (one brother had died) and three girls, Ellen, Clara and Gertrude (my grandmother). Gertrude would have been thought beautiful in Chaucer's day, but not in the nineteenth century or in ours – she had too prominent a forehead. It was probably around 1890 that her cousin, Charlotte, always known as 'Cousin Charl' said to her, in old-fashioned dialect that you would not hear now, 'Gertie, why doesn't thee have a fringe? Theest got a forehead like a monument.' But, as a daughter of the Knight household, Gertrude became a good cook, and learnt, like all the Knights, how to look after money. She was also extremely practical and courageous – she was once sent for from the village to clear out a wasp nest, when nobody else would. She must have been taller than her suitor; and perhaps it is difficult, remembering her dressed in black (women did not wear scarlet to their dying day forty years ago) to think of Gertrude Knight as an object of romance. Except that my wife inherited, from the family, a lovely little Victorian brooch that had been granda's gift to grandma before marriage, all those years ago.

I once had a long talk with a Mr Sylvester Thomas,[1] who as a young man delivered the post at Criggan. "Of course," he said, "the Knights never thrawed nothing away. But they was generous to the postman at Christmas, with handsome Christmas cake especially. I could do good with Granny Knight's Christmas cake now." It was such a background of thrift that grandma, doubtless, needed; for at Higher Trerank the blacksmith and his wife began to raise what used to be called 'a long family'. In more recent times grandma was teased (she did not mind being teased) for having fed the family on stinging nettles (there may have been a grain of truth in this). As a young woman, it was said, her children came too fast, and she had a sort of breakdown. Fortunately, her clever brother Charlie (of whom more anon) was earning a good salary in London and paid for medical attention away from the family. It was part of the treatment that she was made to speak between mouthfuls of food. "But it was all right", said grandma, "if you just said you couldn't think of anything to say".

Returned home, she reared her children and saw them begin to prosper. Selina Crocker, the matriarchal door-to-door gypsy (gypsy queen, perhaps; but I cannot bring myself to call her that, having seen her smoking a pipe in St. Austell Woolworths) Selina would reproach grandma: "You'm too big to buy my clothes-pegs now like you used to. You'm gone up in the world, that's where 'tis to". I cannot imagine that grandma would show remorse by buying more clothes-pegs.

I was checking the proofs for this book when a still better example of what I call Cornubio-Dickensian coincidence occurred. The doorbell at School House, Mount, rang. It was a gipsy selling clothes-pegs and tea-towels. I asked her name: 'Crocker'. What was the name of her husband's grandmother? 'Selina Cocker'. I fetched the passage I had written, about the difference of opinion between a Crocker grandmother and a Phillipps grandmother, of at least sixty years before, and I read it out. Predictably, she did not entirely agree: 'Oh, but grandma was a gipsy queen all right. I remember her driving home to Hensbarrow from the Rock Hotel

---

[1] One of the best antidotes to the process of 'Vanishing Cornwall' so grimly forecast by Daphne du Maurier, is this kind of thing: a friend I met several years ago in Leicester, but from Lanlivery, has gone to live in Roche. There he showed me some furniture that had been left to him by his 'great-uncle Syl'. Who should this be but the late Sylvester Thomas! Unlike my father I am no Dickensian, but this kind of coincidence delights me.

after a Guinness or two, in her pony and trap, going like the Mail.'
I remembered this too; and I yielded the point.

I asked Selina's relative if she lived in a caravan. 'No, in a tent, on St. Neot's downs, now. I've always lived in a tent, and have given birth in a tent. I always gave birth lying on a shock (stook) of corn. That's good luck, dear. I've got grandchildren now; but they weren't born on a shock of corn, owing to the combine harvesters. We used to wash the new-born babies in the stream nearby. That's lovely clean water.'

She looked around at the house appraisingly: 'You wouldn't have any scrap iron, dear? Your father was a very good man for scrap iron. That was when we lived up Hensbarrow. Your father sold my man a big piece of canvas. I think 'twas a rick-cover; old stock. He took it across to the recreation ground on the other side of the road from the shop, and unfolded it.'

'No, I haven't got any scrap,' I said. And then, having invested in a supply of clothes-pegs, I shut the door rather quickly; because I didn't want her to see I was crying. Catching Cornwall in flight can at times be tearful work!

As for grandma, she was more likely to be promoting more ingenious methods of thrift. Many times I have seen her grinding up chicken bones and broken crockery with a hammer, giving the residue to the hens for improved laying. She would get her sons-in-law (but not her sons) to make spills from firewood – you could save as many as four matches a day! Ingenious thrift – it could be a Cornish theme: a Roche man was asked, "What are 'ee savin' your money for? For other people to spend it after you'm gone?" "Well, if they enjoy spending it as much as I've enjoyed savin' it, I shan't begrudge the money."

Grandma had two brothers, Mike and Charlie. Mike emigrated and spent much time in America. He made a deal of money; but he came back to Bilberry, near the ancestral Criggan, to retire. In a remote mountain region of America he had broken his leg, could not get it set properly and so walked with two sticks thereafter.

But Charlie was the *Wunderkind*. At Bugle school, being clever, he stayed on as a pupil-teacher. But, being wise as well as clever, he left teaching and moved to London as a civil servant. At London University, in evening classes, he took a degree in law. Nowadays there would be a host of personal tutors, counsellors, welfare officers and so on. I do not suppose great-uncle Charlie had many of these, but he certainly did well. As became a top civil servant he voted Tory, sending home to his nephews and nieces recently published volumes of Kipling as Christmas presents. He was very scathing of his opponents in the opposite party and especially of the then Liberal Home Secretary, Churchill. "Fancy calling the guard out to a place like Sidney Street!" he said. His powers of intellect and industry (one thinks of Betjeman's line about 'the first class brain of a civil servant') were fully stretched in 1914, when war broke out. He had a bed made up in his office, and he worked there very often into the small hours.

When I knew him, I was a small boy. It was towards the end of his life. He had retired to Highertown, Tremodret, from where he could view his beloved Criggan. If you were taken to visit him he would probably give you an enormous block (bigger than you see nowadays) of Cadbury's chocolate. He would come up to Roche for special occasions like the coronation of George VI in 1937, when the whole village, chapel and church, attended the parish church of St. Gomonda of the Rock. Father said to me, "Don't 'ee make a fuss, but if you get near the church gate, look and see if Uncle Charlie is wearing the medal that the King have giv'd him". So I stood by Roche church gates, and I looked and saw the medal, oval and shining gold. Years later, when studying in a big library, I would on occasion cheer myself up by looking up my great-uncle in an earlier volume of *Who's Who*: KNIGHT, Charles (1860–1941) C.B. 1920. Roche, Cornwall. Assistant Secretary. Local Government Board and Ministry of Health.

Nevertheless, Uncle David told me that his uncle was a disappointed man; he had hoped for a knighthood.

Uncle Charlie lived, in retirement, with his sister Clara and brother-in-law Cap'n George Tippett. Cap'n, of course, in inland Cornwall parlance, means not the captain of a ship, but overseer of a mine or clay works, Uncle George and Auntie Clara had only two children. Did they practise birth control, or was it right, as village wits declared, that on the Sunday following his return from honeymoon Uncle George had preached from the text: 'We toiled all night and caught nothing'?[1] When I was about twelve, Auntie

---

[1] I am often mystified by the extreme discrepancies that occur in such matters; and I am afraid I am not always wise enough to discern the hand of God in them. In contrast to Uncle George was a Roche man with well over a dozen children who was reproached by one of those women ('as sensitive as a goddam toilet seat' in the phrase of J. D. Salinger) who take it upon themselves to order the lives of others: "There's no need of it these days" she said, "you can go chemist's".

" 'Tis no good", said the Roche man. "All I got to do is put my trousers on the bed, and away she go!'

Clara gave me some advice which has remained with me, not so much as wisdom but as a valid generalisation: "We read in the Bible, Kenneth, that money is the root of all evil; but I always think a little of it is handy".

Ellen, grandma's other sister, had four children. With great-auntie Ellen, the culinary skills of the Knight 'maidens' reached their apogee. To go to prosperous Bokiddick farm for Sunday dinner (the word *lunch*, in lower-class circles in the thirties, was used if at all for a mid-morning snack) was to be aware of what farmhouse cooking could be. Best of all, I remember that obsolescent delicacy, the suet pudding soaked in gravy. Even in the West Country the suet pudding has yielded, despite its crisp and tasty brownness, to the insipid batter – from Yorkshire, I suspect.

Auntie Ellen had to a greater degree what all the Knight women had; a tendency to lay great stress on exclamations: as *well! really! goodness!* These words would be pronounced with force from the chest. You could not call it gushing exactly – it was not done to curry favour, but to express enthusiasm.

After dinner at Bokiddick, granda and I would follow Auntie Ellen's husband, John Lobb, to look at the bullocks, and much talk of prices and condition ensued. Granda, mostly retired from blacksmithing and devoting himself to the 'place' (smallholding) was so proud of his animals that he curry-combed them.

Grandma, who had less money than her sisters, went in for plain cooking; and I benefited from this on Roche Fair days (May, July and October) when, owing to the shop being so busy – selling 'nailie' boots in October, for example – I went to Higher Trerank for dinner. The first course would be pasty: 'Let's see,' it would be debated at an earlier stage, 'do Kenneth have onion in his pasty?' 'Yes, Kenneth's very fond of onion in his pasty.' This was enough to arouse some disquiet: no true Phillipps had onion in their pasty; it was perhaps a Hawken tendency. But there was no doubt about my preference in the second course. It was sago pudding; not the large glutinous type of sago so often vilified now but instant nourishment. In Leicester Royal Infirmary recently I found they have some remarkable drugs from which I benefited; but they also have a genius of a cook who cooks sago like grandma's. 'It done me worlds of good!'

Uncle David relates that the school doctor at Newquay County School inquired what he usually had for his lunch. He replied, 'A bun'. A second inquiry the following year elicited the same response. The school doctor sent a memo to Higher Trerank: their son was undernourished. Of course grandma provided nourishing meals, but not at the doctor's lunch-time; at Roche dinner-time! At eighty-five my uncle still cheerfully proceeds on his under-nourished way!

When a religious movement is thriving there seems to be not much attempt to trace its history. People are less interested in origins and the past than in next Sunday's chapel anniversary. Perhaps it is not until fortunes are declining that one tries, as Isaiah recommended, to look 'unto the rock whence ye are hewn'. The Methodism of Trezaise, the chapel in Roche that the Phillippses attended, and where we had (it was a matter of pride to me as a boy) the longest pew, had been Bryanite. William O'Bryan came from another country of hard rock, Luxulyan. To quote the *Oxford English Dictionary*, the Bryanites were 'a protestant sect founded in 1815 by William O'Bryan, a Wesleyan preacher in Cornwall; chiefly in the South-West of England'.

This splinter group from Wesleyan Methodism, the 'Bible Christians' as they came to be called (hence rather misleading dates like B.C.1859 on the outside of chapels) were re-accepted into Methodism in 1907. With the decline of Methodism, it was left to the Rev. Thomas Shaw in his fascinating book *The Bible Christians* to record the growth of the sect, from Luxulyan throughout Cornwall to Devon, London (admittedly in small numbers) etc. There were even missionaries to China!

And all this came from Luxulyan; more particularly from Gunwen, near Helman Tor; still more particularly from Auntie Ellen's farmhouse in Bokiddick; though nobody knew, or at least nobody mentioned this when we went there in the thirties. According to Thomas Shaw, it was in the farmhouse at Bokiddick that God spoke to the eleven-year-old William O'Bryan through the efforts of a local preacher called Stephen Kessell. Only rarely can so much have come from so little. Only rarely can the backwoods have been so elevated.

A year or two ago, talking to cousin Ruby Hugo, Auntie Ellen's daughter at Bokiddick, I said something about Gunwen being an important Bible Christian chapel. She gave me what T.S.Eliot would have called 'a straight look'.

For of course I was wrong. With the cry of 'O'Bryan is about to tear up Methodism by the roots' the Wesleyan Methodists wrested O'Bryan's chapel from him. These 'old unhappy far-off things and battles long ago' may still have slight repercussions. If there is no mid-Cornwall Methodist shrine corresponding to

East Cornwall Trewint and West Cornwall Gwennap, this may be because Wesleyans do not like to be reminded of past misdemeanours. Gunwen remains one of the most interesting chapels in Cornwall.

I remember that when we went to Bokiddick there had to be an early tea for one of the daughters of the household. She had to walk 'a brave little step' to play the organ in the fine two- storey chapel.

At Christmas grandma would give a little party for some of the Knights, her brothers and sisters. Uncle Charlie, his glasses on his forehead, would be there. I would be under ten at the time, present only on suffrance and soon to be fetched home; but with the backward-looking mind of the Celt, I can remember bits of conversation:

"What a mess that fellow Davey has made of Colbiggan. It ought to be a good farm, Colbiggan; enough to raise a family." "Yes, but I think Davey's boy has done very well with moleskins. Do you know, Charlie, you can get as much as a penny a piece for moleskins?"

"But what can you get for a penny these days? You must move with the times, you know, Gertie. But she had that boy before she was married. Now, who was the father? There are quantities of children in Roche these days that I don't know the father of."

So it would go on, with scandals glanced at, illegitimacies canvassed. Not a 'come-by-chance' (to use the dialect word for bastard) could escape.

When, in my teens, I read George Eliot's masterly account of the Dodson family in *The Mill on the Floss*, I recognised that the Knights would have hailed the Dodsons as their kith and kin.

Granda would not be very prominent in this Knights' Christmas party. Perhaps the wealth of Uncle George Tippett was rather intimidating; and of course all the Knights were to benefit when Uncle Charlie died in 1941. Grandma also felt the difference in wealth, but she was reconciled: "Clara can make out a cheque for £100 where I can only make out one for £10; but she won't, so we're 'bout even."

Granda was not without his quiet pleasures. He had even gone off formerly to London occasionally to stay with his brother-in-law Charlie, a bachelor, who had heard a rumour (the time was pre-1914) that suffragettes were going to disrupt the House of Commons. They obtained two tickets of admission; but on that day nothing happened. More frequently, granda would visit his sister Lottie in Plymouth; and once he took me with him. I would be about seven years old, and it was the first time I had crossed the Tamar. In the town, we went upstairs on a bus – an unheard of experience – there were then only single-decker buses in Cornwall. I had also never seen the traffic controlled by coloured lights.

Auntie Lottie, granda's sister and a Trethewey Phillipps, lived in a flat in Plymouth, and this was a surprise; not a bit poky as I had expected. There were big double doors, and a great deal of polished oak. "Does he read, Thomas?" asked Auntie Lottie. "Oh, yes," said granda, "He's a reader all right." "Well, here's the *Children's Encyclopedia*; that'll keep you quiet!" And of course it did. I could never understand why the *Children's Encyclopedia* could be so interesting, while *The Children's Newspaper* by the same editor, Arthur Mee, was so boring!

Auntie Lottie's married name was Stephens, and the family sold cakes, preserves and so on, home-made for the most part. Perhaps their shop would now be a delicatessen. Commercial travellers coming down from Plymouth remembered the business, and talked of it nostalgically, as one of the delights of that joyous pre- blitz, pre-planning city. Auntie Lottie had a largish goitre, covered with a piece of gauze. I suppose goitres can be treated more effectively now.[1]

As I went around the village there were various reminders of the family business. If I visited the home of an elderly couple in Roche and looked at the name above the oven door in the main room, it would probably be J.J.Phillipps, in capitals in cast iron. The stove front would have its name supplied by a Wadebridge Foundry. With a younger couple the name-plate might have T.T.Phillipps. As a small boy, I thought the Phillippses would last for ever. In fact, all the blacksmiths did was fit the stoves in place and see to the flues. 'Exegi monumentum aere perennius', said the Roman poet. (I have erected a monument more lasting than bronze.) All the stoves have since been 'scat up'.

A great preoccupation of most of the Phillipps family has always been reading. Grandma and granda read library books a good

---

[1] It was fascinating to have all this confirmed at this late date by Mrs Jenny Vine of St. Austell (about my age) whom I met recently and who used to visit Auntie Lottie as a Trethewey, not as a Phillipps. Her grandmother, with all the intensity of the Tretheweys, confined her reading to the Bible and the *Christian Herald*. Mrs Vine was also partly brought up by one of the Tippetts and this also gave her the entree to Highertown, Tremodret, where she like me was overawed by Uncle Charlie Knight.

deal, she with one eye shut, for she had a 'lazy eye'. Looking as a boy in the cupboards of Higher Trerank, I found a long run of *The Review of Reviews*, edited by W.T.Stead, a periodical of the turn of the century. I could not make much of the articles, but the cartoons were fascinating.

But there were some books I was not allowed to touch; big, mostly green books, read by granda on Sunday afternoons in winter; with titles like *The Voyage of the Beagle, The Descent of Man*, and *The Origin of Species*. Like many autodidacts, granda had no small talk; once he said to me, apropos of nothing: "Kenneth, Charles Darwin spent seven years of his life studying the earthworm". Darwin was his hero. Granda was born in the eighteen sixties, and I suppose that these books would have represented sensational reading for the thinking man from then until the end of the century, I can imagine him joining in the chapel arguments on the subject at Trezaise, where after morning service the men (I can remember this) would argue about the sermon and related topics; not necessarily too seriously. Some probably would have found granda too arbitrary and irascible (I am like him in this); or, to bring in the essential word to describe us, bigotty.

Chapter 3

The Family

But scorn them not; for they are honest people.
Although perhaps they never saw Paul's steeple

Towards the end of the first decade of this century, a girl in her late teens was leaving her native village of Roche, to start work in service at Carnanton, in the village of Mawgan-in-Pydar. Though she was always top of the class at school, there was no more ambitious opening for her. So although her father in bidding her goodbye said, "Come back home, my dear, if you don't like it", her mother said no such thing.

But Auntie Kathleen (she was my father's eldest sister) stuck it out in the big kitchen of Carnanton. She learnt that as a cook's assistant she had to make as much noise as possible. "Rattle the poker, Phillipps,' she was told, "then they'll think you'm some busy".

Half a century later, when Auntie Kathleen was dead, I told all this to the late Philip Larkin, on one of his frequent visits to Leicester University. He was Librarian of Hull University. He was delighted with the phrase, and often repeated it; "Hull," he said, "is full of noisy, ambitious young men, rattling the poker." It was advice that Auntie Kathleen, at least, did not ignore. You could tell where she was by the clattering of saucepans.

At first Auntie Kathleen was advised to keep her Methodism as inconspicuous as possible; but this as it turned out was unnecessary advice: a few years before, the head of the Carnanton household, Squire Humphrey Willyams, had fallen out with the vicar of Mawgan parish and, according to Charles Lee's journal, for years he mounted his white pony and rode off to the Wesleyan chapel at St. Columb. A Wesleyan squire is a strange phenomenon.

There was said to be a ghost, a spectral coach, at Carnanton, but I do not think that Auntie Kathleen would be troubled by this. "'Tis a fetish," she would say, "like flowers at funerals. Say your prayers and you'll have no trouble." Meanwhile, she made good as a cook, keeping a book of 'receipts', as she called recipes. It is true I only knew her cooking when her career was nearly finished; but it was very good then. At Carnanton and later at Pencrebar she had to cook game, partridge and snipe which were hung and consequently 'high'; "They birds was just about stinkin'; the ordinary run of people don't have to eat muck like that." But even worse to her, as a teetotal Methodist, was that it fell to her to bring in the alcoholic drink. "The worst thing about the gentry," she would say, "is they do tip their elbow so". Many years later, in my own teens, she would subject me to an interrogation:

> You don't drink, do 'ee?
> You don't smoke, do 'ee?
> You don't read Sunday papers, do 'ee?

Her next post was Pencrebar (Callington). It was the home of the Horndons who, like the Hexts of Tredethy, to whom they were closely allied, were a military family. The member of the Horndon family to whom my aunt was most attached, remaining with her for many years, was Miss Nellie Horndon. When, as a consequence of the dwindling of the Horndon family, Pencrebar was sold, Auntie Kathleen moved with Miss Nellie to near Tavistock. Pencrebar was bought in 1927 by a rising Plymouth lawyer with a large family, Isaac Foot. Miss Nellie, a Tory of course, was not at all pleased about the purchaser, and when visiting her sister at Tredethy would go out of her way to avoid the danger of seeing the man she called 'that ranting dissenter'. I wonder what she would have made of Isaac's son Michael and grandson Paul! But Auntie Kathleen was, of course, delighted. Isaac Foot was a staunch Methodist. She had heard him preach.

My best memories of Auntie Kathleen were during the Second World War. Phillipps (Auntie Kathleen's Victorian servant name remained with her throughout her career) was allowed, since she must not leave her aged mistress, to have her nephew and niece to visit. This was at Cross House, Whitchurch Down, near Tavistock. Cross House was what was called a cottage, but it was bigger than almost any house in the china clay villages I came from. All the same, Miss Nellie liked to have her bed shoved up in one corner, to remind her of the still roomier accommodations of Pencrebar.

Miss Nellie did not get up till eleven o'clock or so, when Bertha, the maid, helped her to dress. Very occasionally of an afternoon

Miss Nellie would invite my sister and me into her room, and show us the foxes' heads and brushes, with inscriptions of where the deaths had occurred. "I have always loved outdoor things", said Miss Nellie, who had as a matter of course ridden to hounds in her prime. She explained that there was Sheraton furniture; but perhaps her most valuable possessions were two Tudor jugs, of Barnstaple ware, now donated to Exeter Museum by her nephew, Commander Bush.

I was struck with how far life at Whitchurch Down was like books; very refined of course, and with hindsight rather like that of Miss Marple's St. Mary Mead, of the same period in Agatha Christie's novels. They had all sorts of things we in Roche never dreamed of having, like burglars for example, though we have heard about them since. There was a silver tray for visiting cards, and Bertha, who wore a sort of blue nurse's uniform in the morning for dusting, changed into a brown frock and a black and white taped cap for dealing with calls in the afternoon. This was real life, I thought; and Roche, proletarian Roche, was rather sordid.

I have long decided to reverse that judgement. There is no more boring and baseless virtue than mere refinement; whereas Roche, proletarian Roche, to anybody in the know, is a never-failing source of interest.

At Cross House I slept apart from everybody else, up a separate staircase, in what was called the Studio – a very grand name, I thought: "Well, good night; I'll just go on up to the Studio." Strewn around casually in the Studio were first editions of Dickens – *Dombey and Son*, for example, and *Martin Chuzzlewit*. These would almost certainly have been purchased when published – there was no antiquarian paraphernalia about them. And here were standard Victorian picture books – standard, that is, for those who were well off: *The Comic History of England* and *The Comic History of Rome*.

Each Sunday Auntie Kathleen went at least once, and sometimes twice, to Russell Street Chapel in Tavistock. Tavistock, like Bloomsbury, is full of associations with the Russells, Dukes of Bedford. Before we set off there was often a fuss about the weather: "A bit of a cloud over there," Auntie Kathleen would say. "I'd better take my umbrella."

Auntie Kathleen's ideas on the after-life were clear-cut: "'Tis no use for us to think we'm all goin' to heaven, you know; otherwise heaven would be no better than this place".

On weekdays, we might be summoned to a shopping expedition in Whitchurch Down village. "Come on, my dear Christian friends.

Come on Bertha. Don't stand there on one leg like a stork. We'd better go to the post office for beans." The beans were runner beans, sold at the post office by Joe, on whose account Auntie Kathleen was much teased, not only by Bertha but also by Miss Nellie herself, who though of the bettermost class of people, was also an old maid. Joe had trench feet, a legacy from the First World War. Bertha, however, was keener on a guard on the Yelverton to Tavistock line. The train passed at the bottom of the Cross House garden. She would sometimes let her white apron fly out of the window, and the driver tooted in reply. Auntie Kathleen did not think this was quite the thing. Nor did she mince matters when, my sister, Doreen was elected Roche carnival queen: "'Tis vanity, sheer vanity," she said. Bertha Johns, the maid, protested at this, saying "Well, Miss Phillipps, she was choosed". It will be seen that Bertha never presumed to use my aunt's Christian name. As for her East Cornwall vowel in the word 'choosed', no spelling can do it justice!

But my aunt was too intelligent to be a total killjoy. She was, for one thing, a keen follower of Tavistock's amateur dramatics. We went to see Rattigan's *French Without Tears* and I have rarely laughed so much in a theatre. "We've had our times, Kenneth, you know," she said to me once; and she gave us a good time. The meals were excellent, and if we went on a chapel excursion there might be equally good food, say at Chubb's Temperance Hotel, Callington.

One Phillipps' trait Auntie Kathleen was largely free of: she was not 'near', that is, parsimonious; or perhaps she had acquired from her mistress the habit of stinting herself but being generous to others. Certainly we used to say she bought her hats at jumble sales. She was fond of Miss Nellie, but not blind to her faults. In 1939 Miss Nellie wrote to the defence authorities. She was eighty, she explained, and could not travel far; but if they took her to a depot, she would fill sandbags. ("Stands to reason," said Auntie Kathleen, "they've never done a hand's turn in their life; stands to reason they'm cracky"). Also on the outbreak of war, Miss Nellie decreed there was to be no hoarding of food against rationing. She should have known her Cornwall better. What chance had Whitehall instructions got against a centuries-old desire to hoard and smuggle! If you glamorise smuggling, you cannot then wholeheartedly condemn a black market.

When the war had been going on for some time, Miss Nellie said, "I think it's very clever of you, Phillipps, to manage the food so well."

"The Lord will provide, ma'am," said Auntie Kathleen.

Once, Auntie Kathleen gave me a diary, in good handwriting for the most part, but badly written when the diarist, a Squire Horndon of two hundred years ago, was suffering from gout. The diary, a valuable document for Callington, had been thrown in the bin by an increasingly senile Miss Nellie. I wrote about it in *The Western Morning News*, and received two letters: one from a woman formerly in the Wrens who had been billeted at Cross House. "Your aunt," she told me, "was one of the kindest people I ever knew, and she made the best saffron buns I ever tasted." The other letter was from a Callington researcher, more or less demanding I should pass on the diary. But I think, since Auntie Kathleen had the wit to save it, I shall have the sense to keep it. I thought about this little episode many years later, when I rescued Charles Lee's Journals.

It would be idle to pretend that my aunt had rescued the work of one of the great diarists. Squire Horndon, like Eliza Doolittle in conversation, had mostly two topics – the weather and health: 'Rain the whole day – gout bad; cool dry wind, no frost, gout rather better' To my surprise, I had a touch of gout recently, so I felt for old Squire Horndon, with his crutches and his 'gout shoe' and his occasional visits to Bath when the pain was severe. The Squire's sister, Betsey, booked rooms for him in advance, in Laura Place: a good address, as we learn from reading Jane Austen's *Persuasion*. The squire, a widower, had some relief from his gout in the coach as far as Exeter: an interesting woman 'perhaps between forty and fifty'. He comments: 'I should like to meet her again'.

Always, Auntie Kathleen had the consolations of Russell Street. "I do always like to go twice a Sunday," she would say. "You never know, some time I may be prevented from going." And this happened; the last few years of her life she was the victim of a stroke, in an old people's home.

But I can see her now, going out socialising among her chapel friends. Perhaps it is a Faith Tea; perhaps a bazaar – one of those she worked for. In the lapel of her coat is the Methodist 'shell' and the white ribbon of temperance. Auntie Kathleen did not hide her light under a bushel. As she steps out, she has only one anxiety: "Cloudy. Full's an egg over there, it seems to me. What a good thing I got my mac and umbrella".

The South-West was, until recently, a small world. Auntie Kathleen met in Tavistock an uncle of my mother's, Uncle Walter. He had a shoemaker's business in the town. And where did they meet? In Russell Street Chapel, of course, where Uncle Walter took up the collection, wearing a florid signet ring given to him by his wife, Auntie Bessie for the purpose. He had the staring eyes of the Bates, Grandma Hawken's family. He and his wife used to come and stay in Roche with their niece, my Auntie Ella; she would lay down a thick table-cloth and they would play tiddly-winks. But Auntie Bessie contrived, somehow, to blow the counters, by main force, into the cup; and this dubious finessing nearly caused an international incident between Devon and Cornwall!

Auntie Kathleen did not think very highly of her co-religionist's skill as a shoemaker: "He do trig the heels the way they'm goin'." There is no real equivalent in standard English for this handy word *trig*, meaning something like 'prop'.

Next to Kathleen was Hannah; but she did not go out 'in service'; she was very domesticated, though in youth she had gone down to the village to learn dressmaking; quite a common apprenticeship for young women eighty years ago. She was never strong, and died relatively young; but, up to her fifties, she formed one of a quartette of *maidens* (as mother called them), Phillipps *maidens* who stayed at home and had a lively, not to say noisy, time of it, communally. They turned the hay together, they washed blankets together, they baked hundredweights of cakes and buns together. Their uniform head-dress was a rather unbecoming pixie hood worn long after it became unfashionable. Mother, who was outside the charmed circle, with a place of her own and work to do in the shop, was sometimes rather caustic: "'Ark at 'em: they'm doin' blankets today. Hear 'em scritchin'!" But compared to the neurotic loneliness in which most housework is done in the suburbs, this habit of letting off steam while getting work done was clearly beneficial.

Auntie Hannah's somewhat eccentric and unorthodox style of dress-making consisted in obtaining J.D.Williams's catalogue. Many years later, in Manchester, I passed Messrs J.D.Williams's warehouse, and I felt I was standing on holy ground. Auntie Hannah would measure the customer, send for the material and cut out the dress, or whatever, from the picture. This was not always very successful, and my sister Doreen, to whom clothes were very important, at the age of about fifteen staged a rebellion. She was not going to wear any more of Auntie Hannah's old things. Surprisingly, perhaps because Hannah was not his favourite sister, father took Doreen's side: "I don't see why the chield shouldn't wear what she've a mind to."

But between Auntie Hannah and me there was, when I was

26

young, quite a partnership. When I was really small, so I am told, I was sometimes allowed to turn the handle of her sewing-machine. A little older, as I was helping her to 'feed the fowls', Auntie Hannah said to me: "When you grow up and write a book, Kenneth, you will have to call fowls' dung, chicken's droppings". The eighteenth century poet Thomson writes of teaching 'the young idea how to shoot'. I have written several books, but have never mentioned chicken's droppings until now.

A keen Methodist in youth, Auntie Hannah led a well-regulated life. Much in her occupations was prescribed. Even the Bible she read in bits, through the Scripture Union. For me, she bought *The Clarion* 'for Western wideawakes'. This was the junior Journal of the Western Temperance League, emanating from Bristol. Not much publication is based in the South-West now, but Auntie Hannah's favourite newspaper, *The Western Morning News*, is edited from Plymouth still. It is said that an Exeter woman councillor, a good many years ago, disagreed violently with her opponents at a meeting of the city council, and called out "Knickers!". Nearly all the local papers reported this – except *The Western Morning News*. I can see Auntie Hannah reading the chaste columns of this paper. It is propped up against the secretaire (*secoteer* we called it, perhaps by confusion with *secateur*) – that is, when there are no buns on it. Buns are, or were, very important in Cornwall. She is warming her hands on a cup of tea she is holding, standing on one leg.

Apart from a period as Uncle Charlie's housekeeper in London, Auntie Hannah led a limited life, which is summed up for me in something she wrote in my autograph book:

> For every evil under the sun
> There is a remedy or there's none.
> If there's a remedy, try to find it,
> If there's none, try not to mind it.

When I came back to Roche at Christmas after my first term as an undergraduate in Liverpool, she said, "'Tis surprising how much more interest we take in Liverpool and the North of England when we read about these places in the papers now". A few months later she was dead.

A third aunt was Edith. Auntie Kathleen, her elder sister, being sometimes subject to fits of jealousy, used to say to me, "Really, I suppose your Auntie Edith is your favourite auntie, isn't she, Kenneth?" The temptation to say 'Yes' was too strong to be resisted. But in any case she was. When my sister was very ill I stayed with Auntie Edith and her husband, Uncle Owen, for a few weeks.

Auntie Edith had a rather bitter tongue, but a kind heart. I am afraid that, intellectually, she was the weakest of the Phillipps family of that generation. For instance, she would mix up *privet* and *pivot*, which could be disconcerting: "We'd better cut down some of that pivot". One of the funniest dialect exchanges I remember occurred when the scholarly rector of Roche, John Tarplee, came to collect Auntie Edith's glebe rent, She had a loud voice and he easily overheard her. "I lost three libraries," said Auntie Edith, "Ethel M.Dell. I don't know where they'm to". "Excuse me, Mrs Paynter," said the parson, "everybody in Roche seems to make the same mistake. A library is not a library book. *Liber* is Latin for 'book', and *librarius*, is the derived form. After all, a library can contain thousands of books." As soon as he was out of earshot Auntie Edith began: "I sometimes think these here parsons and rectors and that, I sometimes think they ain't none of 'em zackly. What did I say? All I said was I lost three libraries. I shall have some fine to pay if I don't find 'em soon."

Auntie Edith may not always have used proper words in proper places; but she had one undoubted talent. She was a natural rearer; that is to say, she could enhance the process of growing in humans, beasts and plants. She raised young turkeys very successfully, feeding them on meal fortified with hard-boiled eggs (I have since wondered about the profit margins). She reared calves, putting her hands into their mouths under their shiny noses to make sure they were 'zucking' properly. From one Christmas berry (solanum) she gave away each Christmas several plants she had brought on from it. And of course, for the time that I stayed with her she reared me. Every morning she would bring from the dairy for our 'crib' a rich cup of 'raw milk' as we called it, that is milk not yet scalded for cream. But she herself had a cup of coffee.

We have got very pernickety about coffee now. For Auntie Edith coffee came as a strong undiluted liquor in a big bottle. This was Camp coffee with chicory. On the bottle was a picture of a mustachioed Scottish warrior in a kilt, with bare knees. He was sitting drinking coffee; and this had been brought in by a turbaned Indian – I expect he was a sepoy – carrying a tray. On the tray was a bottle of Camp coffee; on the bottle in miniature was a Scottish warrior in a kilt, waited on by a sepoy . . . I was intrigued that this process could go on for ever, and I explained it all to Auntie Edith as we sat drinking. She was not a bit impressed at the idea of holding infinity in the palm of her hand in the shape of a bottle of Camp coffee with chicory. Instead she looked worried: "Come on, Kenneth, this won't do , we shall have you bad next. We'd better go and pick up eggs".

Few activities are as therapeutic as picking up eggs. The search is challenging, the goals are easy to achieve. Auntie Edith's hens had an orthodox fowls' house with orthodox nesting-boxes attached. It was a Harry Hebditch; supplied, of course, by C.T. Phillipps. But the hens were true nonconformists and made their nests as they liked; in last year's hayrick, up the hedge-banks, all over the place. One of my jobs was to go to the cows' house, when suddenly there might be a flutter and a clatter and a hen would come out of a bucket leaving an egg. The farmyard was not large; but nevertheless a hen would sometimes contrive to make herself scarce for a long time. Then she would suddenly appear, leading a couple of chicks; not in the least abashed. The dialect comment was: 'She've stole her nest'. The eggs would be collected for Mr Algar, who bought them wholesale. Mr Algar was a regrater. I did not encounter this word again till I read the fourteenth century poem *Piers Plowman*. The meaning remains roughly the same.

It was no wonder that the family as a whole liked Auntie Edith even though she had a temper and also panicked when the phone rang (especially when Uncle Owen was on standby for the Electricity Board and had to be fetched quickly from 'down the garden' – a portentous event). The Phillipps family showed their affection for Auntie Edith in the usual way, by 'jawing'. "'Tis time you got rid of that cold" Uncle David would scold. "You've had it for ages. You'm cough, cough, cough, cough all the time. I got this trade for 'ee from the chemist's. Mind you do exactly what it say on the packet; three times a day!"

In middle age Auntie Edith put on a great deal of weight. One day my wife, Pat, and I watched as she stood framed in the doorway of her cottage, motionless. Suddenly my aunt raised her hand. Pat was reminded of Galileo's words about the movement of the globe: 'E pur si muove' – yet it does move. However, Auntie Edith defied the doctors by living to the age of eighty-one with very high blood-pressure. She did not take to her diet. Ordered to eat more lettuce she rebelled, as anybody might, and fell back on her favourite food which was cake. Not of course 'boughten' cake; she was an excellent maker of home-made cakes: saffron cake, white yeast cake, marble (multi-coloured) cake, seedy cake – all these and more she baked with great skill in the old days, before the Weight Watchers inveighed against such pleasures. Then the

29

Cornish had had an unchecked love for what in dialect is called 'cakey-trade'. One day in the middle of the week was baking day; there was a delicious smell to remind you of the fact as you came to the back door. I remember Auntie Edith coming in to Grandma's when the secretaire was piled high with cakes, etc. She exclaimed: "Lor, you got enough here for Kitchener's army!" Kitchener went down with the *Hampshire* in 1916, but he lingered in the dialect some thirty years more.

At an earlier stage in the baking the dough would have been put in quite large pans in front of the kitchen range, 'to plum'; that is, to cause the warmed yeast to swell the dough. The standard English word for this is 'to prove'. Once it was plum, 'lovely and plum' as the phrase was, the swollen dough needed to be kept warm, perhaps with an overcoat thrown over it. But one method used in far Littlejohns near Hensbarrow was to put the pan of dough in the bed to keep it plum; this was frowned on in more sophisticated places like Roche.

Auntie Edith cooked savoury food also, for Uncle Owen. There was nothing of the frugality of the Phillipps in Uncle Owen's diet. They had a dairy and he loved cream – not only with bread and jam, and brown sugar, but also poured on vegetables: turnips, beans etc., in short, with everything except pilchards: 'cream on pilchards' means anything overdone, in bad taste. The Phillipps family, of course, turned up their noses at such rich food: "They'll suffer for it with their stomach, later; they'll wish their cake dough". Yet the Paynters lived a disconcertingly long time.

I am very grateful to Auntie Edith for training me in gardening, giving me plants from her greenhouse, and telling me off when I was neglecting them. Later in life I found gardening an antidote to school teaching, in so far as there is an antidote; for the most part I define teaching in a school as being 'tied to the bull's ass and shit to death', as they say in Cornwall. From Uncle Owen, in my short stay with him, I learnt to fold up and organise my clothes (father dropped all his on the floor). Uncle Owen liked to take me with him (I was about ten at this time) when he took the cow to the bull at Tregarrick farm. Tregarrick is Celtic for 'place of the Rock' and so, many years later, I chose it as my name as a Bard of the Gorsedd. The affair with the bull cost half a crown a time; and I was very interested in it, as also in the mating of rabbits in the hutches at the side of Uncle Owen's garden: ("and if the buck don't kick on leaving the doe, tid'n young rabbits".)

In old age and as a widower, the forcefulness that had made

Uncle Owen the leader of an outdoor gang working for 'the Electric' turned to obstinacy and random irritability. When the ninth Lord Falmouth, for instance, raised the rent of Uncle Owen's small- holding to what was probably a more economic level (for years he had paid 7/- a week), my uncle was beside himself with rage: "The bugger is overcharging me shameful for rent. I got to pay it. Well, all I know is, he shan't have no rhubarb. There's a handsome lot of rhubarb. I'll creesoe (creosote) the rhubarb!" Which he did forthwith.

Uncle Owen had a little car – an A35, a model which may now have a certain idiosyncratic extra value, especially in the South-West where the combustion engine is king.[1] When he had to give up driving he sold his car at what was probably not a very advantageous price.

What follows is purest Roche. His neighbours, not without malice, told Uncle Owen: "You could have got a purdy lot more for your car than what you did. You was done down there sure 'nough". Uncle Owen then decided that he would obliterate such an unacceptable memory by burning down the garage the car had been kept in. Then to his fury my sister, who lived next door, very reasonably thought it safer to report the blaze to the Fire Brigade: "That bugger Doreen – she would make a fuss like that!"

I can just imagine the news going from the Rock Hotel to the other pub: "Do you knaw what he've done? Just because I said he never got a fair price for his car!"

Auntie Alice I have mentioned before; a woman of incisive intelligence who has regularly commented on my radio broadcasts: "Kenneth, what is this nonsense about *kiddly-broth*? *Kiddly* is *kiddly* and *broth* is *broth*. Which do you mean?" (She is only partly right, because in some parts of the county they speak of *kiddly-broth*, whereas in mid-Cornwall, as she says, *kiddly* is bread and milk, while *broth* has a meat base). She does make rather a speciality of fine-line distinctions in this way. She was mentioning a Roche youth who had gone to gaol, but had made good there, so much so that he had been promoted to the rank of 'trusty'. A trusty, I wanted to know, was that something similar to a trustee?

---

[1]   In East Cornwall, especially, not to own a car is to number oneself among the deprived classes. As the oldest inhabitant of Mount said, of a certain newcomer: 'Who's that man with thick glasses, wolken everywhere, wolken! Aven'a got no car?'

"No, Kenneth", said Auntie Alice firmly, "a trusty is not a bit like a trustee!" For years she was extremely careful and saving, but inflation has killed this, as she herself admits: "I used to be as tight as Jackson (a Jackson wrench), but I don't care now. It used to take years to save a thousand pounds; now a thousand pounds is hardly worth saving anyway". She is a widow and was married to Uncle Gordon, brother of Uncle Owen. Uncle Gordon was a devotee of his male voice choir, and liked to tell me about the latest 'pieces' they were singing: "*Vital Spark*, Kenneth, that's a handsome piece; but 'tis funny time, that's the only thing; funny time."

Uncle David was the only one of this generation of Phillippses to be educated beyond the age of fourteen, at Newquay County School, later training as a teacher at Exeter. I have often thought, as I struggled with poorly motivated students at Leicester University, that at least three others of his brothers and sisters with no such privilege, Auntie Kathleen, Auntie Alice and my father would also have done well. Uncle David is now well over eighty. His daughters have distinguished themselves in teaching, and local government (Mrs Lorna Yelland). I remember him in the thirties as a young teacher, constantly active, gardening, working at postal courses in art, in craft, and so on. He taught me a little bit of French one evening, and since the school doctor came the next day, I repeated the words to him: 'Les Trois Ours'. *Immenso giubilo* from the infant school mistress. Uncle David was probably the fittest of that generation, physically. I remember him jumping the big white garden gate with ease.

He was an advocate of corporal punishment; and who shall say in view of recent horrendous juvenile violence, that he was wrong? When corporal punishment became unfashionable and eventually illegal he still kept a cane hanging in his classroom. Those who taught under him have spoken of him as both just and dignified; a dignity enhanced by his never wearing a sports jacket in school, always a dark suit. I think this propriety came from his father, whom he now strongly resembles facially. It was a quality that my own father did not inherit.

But outside the classroom, and when socialising, Uncle David was not so fond of formality. An exasperated Auntie Joan, his wife, used to say: "The trouble with David is that he won't go anywhere where he can't take his teeth out." Faced with the prospect of some horrible stiff university occasion where cheerfulness was enjoined I have often thought of my uncle and of my aunt's phrase.

Uncle David always found his father difficult to communicate with; granda could show more affection for me I suppose because of the generation between. Uncle David describes a sequel to a very serious motor cycle accident in which through no fault of his he was seriously injured and his fiancée, the pillion passenger, killed. Granda, obviously very distressed, came to the Plymouth hospital where his son was as quickly as he could in those days. He immediately went to the bedside and kissed his son. Uncle David was in his early twenties; "I never realised till then that my father loved me", he said.

Conversation with Cornish people over the age of eighty can at times be only too predictable: "'Tis some different from what 'twas backalong. And of course everything is heaps dearer, compared to what it used to be."

Conversation with my octogenarian uncle and aunt does not follow this pattern very closely: "Of course, if there's any offence I shall sue," says my uncle. "That's all 'bout that. I shall sue."

"I see you'm wearing cords again," says my aunt. (She disapproves of corduroy for menswear) "What do 'ee think you are? A farm labourer?"

However, I would not have it supposed that I am not on good terms with my relatives.

The word for the last, smallest and weakest pig of a litter (*runt* in standard English) is in mid-Cornwall a *nestle-bird*; and the word can apply to people; it could apply to the last Phillipps of her generation, Auntie Ethel. She was born on January 11th, 1914. I remember the date because another baby girl, named Mary Hill, was born in Roche on the same day and the doctor came to her first, so Mary Spear has told me. Mary Hill is now the widow of Ruskin Spear, the portrait painter. The Hills were not perhaps the 'bettermost class of people' since they were in trade, but they were a cut above the Phillippses; not least because they were prosperous enough to educate Mary at home, with the aid of a governess. It seems incredible that there should have been a governess in Roche, the most plebeian village in Cornwall; but the photographs Mary showed me cannot lie.

Auntie Ethel was delicate, and somewhat precocious. A family anecdote relates that they were teasing her, suggesting they got rid of her. She was, it seems, about five; and she replied: "You got me and you got to keep me; the Lord's name be praised" (praiséd on two syllables). I have heard this story too often to be sceptical about it. She never really took to women's work, but liked cutting *dashels* (thistles) and gardening. But she too, as a Phillipps, had certain intellectual aspirations. For years she ran the outpost of the county library, which opened weekly at the school.

Later she went in frantically for knitting, and once knitted me an extremely long Liverpool University scarf. It was too long to be practical, a terrible waste of wool; but it answered something eccentric in both our natures.

Auntie Ethel's favourite tea-time food was Youma, an oblong malt loaf. She would cut off six or eight slices for her tea, spread them generously with butter and make her way inside the long table at Higher Trerank, with a 'library' also in her hand. In the circumstances she had no inclination to talk. She also used to read a novelette-type periodical, 'The Red Letter', probably the trashiest women's journal of the time. When I got older and cheekier, I told her 'The Red Letter' was rubbish. "Don't you criticise 'The Red Letter', she said. "It's next in literature to the Bible".

Auntie Ethel loved pets, and was usually accompanied by a dog. As she grew older the dog tended to be a poodle, held on her arm. When Pat and I were in Roche on holiday, she would come in: "Hullo, Judy, they'm home again. Are they all right, do you think?" Correct protocol was to reply through the dog: "Hullo, Judy. How's Auntie Ethel? Both of 'ee all right?"

At one time she sported an elaborate arrangement of small curls, taking endless time to set in place. Once, when playing hockey (it was one of her accomplishments), she was dismayed because the rain had unravelled all the curls. There was only one dialect phrase that would fit the bill, and mother used it: 'like an owl looking out of an ivy bush.'

When I was about fifteen I went to Auntie Ethel's wedding to Lewis Cross, which was held in Zion Bible Christian Chapel, St. Austell, a rather shabby backstreet building; fallen glory, in fact. I learnt that day that this Bible Christian chapel was the traditional place of marriage for the Phillippses; partly because the Roche chapels were not until fairly recently licensed for the solemnisation of marriage. In general, before 1907 and amalgamation, Zion must have been the place of marriage for a wide area; though there was also in St. Austell a more opulent Wesleyan building, now called St. Johns. Uncle Lewis was a railwayman and in the lapel of his coat was a badge: 'Workers of the world, unite'. He was perhaps the only member of that generation of the family to vote Labour. The Phillippses, in the past at least, did not think it was quite the thing! He worked at a signal-box at Tregoss on the Newquay branch line; but as he generally took with him a radio and one or two 'libraries', presumably the work was not very strenuous. But he was very fond of Auntie Ethel, and when she died before three score years and ten, he soon followed.

I have left my father to the last of the Phillippses of his generation, despite the fact that he was outstanding in personality, and the one local people still most remember. He was not the eldest son since his brother Frank died young of cancer; but he was destined to be the heir, to live eventually in Job's house and to carry on the blacksmith's trade.

My mother was in the same class at the village school and found him exasperating. Mr Dempster, head of the school, used to say: "Put your hand down, Charles; we know you know the answer." ("He only pretended to know", said mother.) But he could not but be aware that he was well above the average intelligence; not in regard to his blacksmith's craft, I suspect, nor in the normal run of ways by which prowess is achieved in a village. His skills were largely verbal. My wife Pat remembers her first meeting with him. He had just come from his cement store and was covered in cement dust. When she was introduced to him, he made a mistake in conversation; "That was a *lapsus linguae* as you educated people call it, isn't that right?" Not many in Roche would have known what he meant. He sometimes mispronounced words he had merely read in books: *hyperbole* rhymed with *coal*; but I never knew him use words in wrong places.

Whereas his father had been interested in natural history, Charlie was keen on politics. After all, the thirties when he was in his prime was a great decade for politics. Every Wednesday in winter when I was a small boy, I remember him coming upstairs and putting on a dickey, that is a detached shirt front, so that he did not have to change his working shirt. With this and a ready-tied tie (he was very bad at tying ties) attached to the shirt by a stud, he went to a W.E.A. class run by a Mr Martin, who later taught me history, and whose son was until recently the Vice-Chancellor of Newcastle University (Sir Laurence Martin). The rector of the village, John Tarplee, must have found most of his Anglican congregation less than stimulating, and was a great friend of my father's. He handed on copies of *The Spectator* regularly, and always gave him a book for Christmas.

One year the book was Sir Edmund Gosse's *Father and Son*; I remember them both chuckling over the confession of the son, narrowly brought up, about having eaten a forbidden piece of Christmas pudding: 'Father, I have eaten of the flesh offered to idols'.

Mr Tarplee had no opinion of the sometimes grotesque narrow-mindedness of some chapel-goers. Of one such man, called by the unfortunate but actually rather common Cornish name of Blight, he said he thought he was "Blight by name and Blight by nature".

Like Uncle Will, his brother-in-law, father could be very amusing. One incident happened in war-time, when Auntie Edith decided to diversify her life by papering a bedroom with the variegated contents of a wallpaper pattern book. For good measure she painted the iron bedstead with aluminium paint. "Charlie and Kenneth," she said, "come up and see what I've done to my bedroom." As we entered the room father whispered to me: "So He giveth His beloved sleep." "What are you laughing at, Kenneth?" Auntie Edith asked. I could not explain.

Mother was a foil for his wit. Once she talked of an illegitimate son who looked after his mother well: "These children are sent for a purpose, sent for a purpose", said mother. "I am sorry," said father, "that I am now too old to take full advantage of the freedom which your last remark apparently gives me!"

As a young woman mother was very thin. When she was over eighty and a widow she told me with a twinkle in her eye: "Your father said to me once: 'You'm some thin, maid. I tell 'ee, a few more navels and you'd pass for a bravish tin whistle!'"

Father was strong on repartee, something in which I am sadly deficient. When the aforementioned affair of the fireworks became more widely known, an old man said to him: "Here, what's this about all they fireworks wasted?" "Well," was the reply, "one thing, there was nobody hurted – nobody hurted." The old man in question, decades before, had been partly concerned with the collapse of a brickwork kiln, with much injury.

It is for this kind of repartee, not to say cheek, that my father is still remembered. It is not a Phillipps' characteristic, and I asked my last surviving uncle about it: "Your father, Kenneth, was not a Phillipps; he was a Knight."

I was still not satisfied; for as far as I knew the Knights were not cheeky either. Uncle Charlie earning his medal from the King, Uncle Mike making his fortune in the Rocky Mountains? I appealed to my last surviving aunt. "Your father was cheeky like your great-grandfather my granda Knight". Auntie Alice could not conceal a certain residual sense of shock as she told me of something that had happened seven decades before: "Granda Knight was even cheeky to Cap'n Arthur!"

It gradually transpired that Cap'n Arthur gave my great-grandfather the sack.

I remember that as late as the nineteen thirties, if anybody had done something particularly reprehensible, such as pleasuring on the beach on a Sunday,[1] the cry would go up "What would Cap'n Arthur say?" It must be borne in mind that a clay cap'n (and I gather he was every inch a clay cap'n) had power to hire or fire any man in his workings. If, in addition, he was a leader in chapel society, and a strong personality to boot, the result was a formidable challenge, I suppose, to my great-grandfather's impudent wit.

My mother's family, the Hawkens, came from the north coast, Little Petherick and St. Issey, in the neighbourhood of Padstow. How they came from there to the china clay area has been told by my mother's brother, the late Captain Harold Hawken, to Kenneth Hudson and quoted verbatim in Hudson's *History of English China Clays*. Talking of movement from farming to clay because of depression in agriculture, Cap'n Hawken, born in Little Petherick, states:

My father used to drive a corn-wagon out here to mill the corn, back in they days. He got married and the wages was 12s 6d a week. Well, seeing he got married, the farmer thought, well, he wouldn't be so independent, so he cut'n 6d a week. Instead of 12s 6d he had 12s 0d. Well then he used to bring corn out here to a man called Marshall, who had an interest in clay, and he offered him a job, so he picked up when I was two years old and came out here.

'Here' would probably be Whitemoor, where my mother was born; and then on to Roche.

But my granda, William Hawken, mentioned here as a waggoner, himself had a father living, back in St. Issey near the Ring of Bells. It may be that the Ring of Bells was my Hawken great-grandfather's downfall. All my mother remembered was being taken in a wagonette, as a small girl, to St. Issey, and hearing my great-grandfather call out from inside his house: "Is that you, William? Come in. Don't let the children see me like this." No doubt it would be a desolate interior – a scene reminiscent of Thomas Hardy. It was total ostracism, in this Cornish village

---

[1] The word does not necessarily mean what it would inevitably mean now. It was genuinely shocking, in Methodist circles, to play with a beach ball on Sunday by the seaside.

at the turn of the century, when the consensus was all for righteousness leading to success. The same note is struck in my great-grandfather's nickname, which was Winter Hawken; I cannot imagine a more evocative but chilling name. What had he done? Mother was evasive. "He served my grandmother some bad; she was a Boscombe".

Not very long ago I took the bus from Bodmin Parkway to Padstow, and the route was via St. Issey. I got into conversation with a woman, and asked her about my great-grandfather, expecting little. But it seems it was a nickname not to be forgotten: "Winter Hawken," she said, "oh, yes, I've heard the name. 'Course, 'twas long before my time, but I've heard of 'un. Ghastly old beggar, I've heard."

If Roche had been a residential area in 1900 (which it isn't even now, being for one thing mercifully free from stuffiness) the place Granda Hawken chose to bring up his children in would have been the most exclusive in the village. It was on the banks of the stripling Fal; his cottage was called Riverside. To quote word for word from the Leeds Dialect Survey for Cornwall: 'We do call 'em all rivers; they aren't but streams'. The place was called Reeshill; and its chief claim to fame was, and I suppose still is, the Reeshill Shoot, with its exceptionally clear and fine-tasting drinking water. Further up the valley is Colvreath, where there was a pony tied up, that the Hawken children used to untie and ride: "'Tis a wonder we didn' break our necks," mother used to say. Still further up is Pentonvale or Pentevale, the name of which to the Celticist is self-explanatory: *pen* meaning head and *fenton* meaning spring – 'Head spring of the Fal'. Here mother, who did not have auburn hair for nothing, fell out with her friend Kitty Ellis and hit her over the head with a bottle of milk. ("I got into some trouble over that milk" she said.)

Reeshill was a good place to rear what used to be called in the South-West 'a long family'; and the Hawkens were all of them strictly brought up. "Father," said my mother, "used to hit us, when necessary, over the head with the edge of his flat cap; and it was surprising how much it hurt . . . Two of us children would take it in turns to go to the other room on Sundays to eat our dinner on the *flour 'itch* (flour hutch, chest for flour), and we used to fight for that freedom from control". There would, of course be no luxuries. Mother's eldest brother, Uncle Will, told me that it was the job of the big boys to bring in a supply of '*vuzz*' (furze bushes) to keep the fire going; and since these were dragged across the earth (not concrete) floors, we can imagine the mess.

When one remembers, in Victorian novels, genteel prejudice against 'trade', it is worth recalling from casual remarks made in Roche that this could work the other way. Mother's family was a labouring family; I have heard her say many times that 'the Hawkens wasn't good for nothing more'n louster' – hard labouring work. The Phillipps's fortunes (for good or ill) were based not so much on 'trade' as on 'a trade'. They gave estimates, they kept accounts, they sent in bills. Such activity had a certain status. To Lilian Hawken, walking to work down Roche Hill, passing the shop where the man she later married would be working, it might have seemed a step up from working in Roche Co- op for an initial wage of 2/6 a week (though she was soon promoted). But, she explained to me, you had to hurry on, because if Tom Phillipps was in one of his 'ghastly' moods, "he might thraw the hammer at 'ee" – but here I think she was joking.

I like to think of my mother's father as a waggoner around Little Petherick – a tranter, Thomas Hardy would have called him. The Hawken facial characteristics are thin lips, prominent eyebrows and auburn hair; all of which my mother inherited. She also inherited his strong constitution. A grandson of his boasted, "I'm goin' to last because I've got a Hawken heart, not a Yelland heart." He was wrong; he died in middle age a few weeks later.[1]

Bill Hawken senior was not in the least like the Phillippses; if there was no great brain, there was also no intellectual top-hamper, no biggottiness to hinder being hail-fellow-well-met with everybody. He enjoyed beer; and did without it if he couldn't afford it, for he was a responsible family man. It may have been his liking for beer that caused him to change from chapel to church (beer was very much a doctrinal issue sixty years ago). He also took to bell-ringing too – but that might be expected from a St. Issey man.

Though Fanny, his wife, was my grandmother I did not know her well. She was a good cook; but most women were in those days. 'Stand by your man' is currently a rather silly ballad; sixty years ago women sensed that it was more important to feed him! As my father (who being a Phillipps did not like food much) used

---

[1] I did not know my cousin, Derek Hawken, well but he was what they used to call a 'buster' (lively man). When mother and father were both approaching eighty he told them: "You realise you'll be promoted now. You'll join the ranks of the 'marvellous reellies'. They'll say, 'He's marvellous reelly'!"

to say "Most men are tied like bullocks by the mouth". Fanny was good at growing flowers; but Roche was 'rough and cold' compared to Little Petherick. She was very short-sighted and this, it was said, was because her parents had not drawn the blinds or curtains when she was in bed with measles as a little girl. When I had measles I was in deep darkness for days to ward off this calamity. Grandma's ears were pierced in the hope that this would also improve her sight. She was a great believer in folk remedies, a great frequenter of Auntie Em. Auntie Em lived in Rosennanon, a remote part of the remote parish of St. Wenn. Her full name was Emily Pryne, and she was gifted, provided you believed in her charms, with the power of removing ringworms or warts. I think that 'Auntie' is a courtesy title, given by those who are not necessarily kin, but in affection and respect. We were always assured that Auntie Em was a 'goodliving' (i.e. virtuous) woman; she read the Bible over the affected part. "When she finished reading the Bible over my ringworm", my cousin told me, "my hand was red hot".

I do not think that Auntie Em tackled anything beyond minor ailments. For one reason or another, I do not think that she would have tackled impotence, as some exceptionally powerful charmers have been known to do.

All in all, it is clear that Grandma Hawken, like all her family, was a woman-of-the-people type. The Phillippses, on the other hand, were never men-of-the-people people. This is in no way a political comment; it was partly that the Phillippses went their own way and did not 'take in' tabloid newspapers.

My cousin, Mrs Kathleen Snell, a daughter of Uncle Will, provided me with an evocative picture of their later life 'out Council'. Grandma Hawken announces, "Well, I must gone on up and ent (empty) the pots into the slop-bucket. If I don't make haste I shall have Allie Gregory in here, blocking the way with her big breastes."

I doubt if you would hear anything equivalent to that last word now. In earlier dialect words ending in 'st' formed their plural with an extra syllable: words like 'clothes-line postes' and 'birds' nestes'.

To turn now to mother's brothers and sisters, Uncle Tommy, one of the older ones, can soon be dealt with; he was killed in the First World War; 'And he never ought to have gone,' I can still hear a chorus of Hawkens lamenting, 'he was short-sighted and below military age.' I have heard this many times. I have never heard 'Of course as a family we are proud he died for King and Country'. For Dr Johnson, patriotism was the last refuge of a scoundrel; to the working-class Cornishman, perhaps with a job, perhaps even with that prized possession 'a little place out of coor', patriotism would have seemed the last refuge of an idiot. I have often thought that this anti-jingoism had at least one advantage, in that it prevented the far South-West from being uniformly Tory; even today there are two Liberal M.P.s. Uncle Tommy, according to mother, was 'an aggravating tawd' (toad), but you couldn't help liking him; even though he would '*stank* (stamp) our marbles in the earth'. If he said "Lil, I'll give 'ee a penny if you'll clean my shoes,' you knew if you cleaned them you wouldn't get a penny.'" And this would have put mother into a dilemma because she had a curious addiction to cleaning shoes. As for the question of patriotism and the classes in Cornwall, this has been brilliantly dealt with by Geoffrey Grigson, in the penultimate chapter of his autobiography, *The Crest on the Silver*.

Geoffrey Grigson tells how, at the beginning of the war, his mother talked to a working-class woman Florrie, who had known all seven of the Grigson boys. Mrs Grigson was not pleased when Florrie talked about the exemption of her own men-folk from war service. Mrs Grigson said she would like all her sons to go, and would be very proud if they died for their king and country. As can be seen from the memorial tablet in the church of Pelynt where Geoffrey's father was vicar, only one son, Geoffrey, survived.

Uncle Harold, Cap'n Harold Hawken, mentioned before, was older than mother and she did not particularly like him: "He tell lies faster than a 'oss can gallop". This was not accurate; but mother hated even the temporary untruths essential to leg-pulls. I re-member during the war, in 1940, when rumours were rife, that he came out with "There was a landmine dropped near Prosper. Two gypsies was killed – blowed to smithereens. But yet they knawed they was gypsies!" "How did they knaw they was gypsies?" A long pause. We had swallowed the bait. "Well, see, they knawed they was gypsies be the clothes-pegs stuck up their ass".

Auntie Louie was the eldest of mother's sisters. She had married Uncle Charlie Roberts (always so called to distinguish him from other Uncle Charlies), and he worked at the wolfram mine at Castle-an-Dinas until a combination of asthma and 'the dust' made him a semi-invalid. Not that he remained inactive. I suppose that by instinct he was always a poacher, and they said that all the family of five boys was brought up on rabbit pie. So far as I know, he was only in trouble once with the law. This was when he shot a fox when the hounds were in full cry after it! A long time afterwards he summed up the affair to me: "Spoiled their sport, see boy. Didn't like it. Fined me thirty shellen". From the look in

Uncle Charlie's eye you could see that it was money well spent. No one could call Uncle Charlie dull. With his sons he used to play what they called 'the music'. They played mandolins, guitars and so forth, long before Lonnie Donegan promoted guitars and washboards to a higher musical level.

Auntie Louie I liked, though I don't think she really approved of me. She looked very like her mother, grandma Hawken, with straight hair. Like her mother she wore her beret down to just above her eyebrows. Once, one fine summer evening, I went for a walk on the Goss Moor, and came to St. Wenn council houses. Auntie Louie was standing outside her home.

"Hullo," she said, "you home?"

"Yes", I said, "I've finished with college".

"About time too," she said. "You won't be an expense to your mam and dad any more. Well, what be 'ee goin' do? Teach? Where be 'ee goin' teach? Up Nottingham?" (Only roughly that; but it would have taken too long to explain) Auntie Louie pounced on this point; "What's wrong with all the schools round here?"

I muttered something about going to teach in the Midlands. She tried another tack. "You don't go in 'cross no wrasslin', I s'pose?"

"No, Auntie Louie," I said. "I have never gone in for wrasslin'"

(St. Wenn and St. Columb have always been great centres for wrestling.)

"You should have gone wrasslin.' 'Twould keep 'ee fit, you know."

It was curious. During my last year at university I had studied *The Republic* of Plato. He too had advocated wrestling to offset strenuous mental effort. It was strange that the thinking of Plato and the thinking of Auntie Louie should so coincide.

Auntie Louie continued: "All five of my boys have won a belt for the wrasslin'. Billy, the best of 'em, just about thrawed Sid Chapman". I was subdued to silence. Though leading a retired life, I was not so ignorant of the world that I had not heard of Sid Chapman, who had won enough belts to keep the whole of St. Columb town free from anxiety about their wrasslin' shorts for all time. As for me, I should go down in history merely as the man whose cousin had 'just 'bout thrawed' Sid Chapman.

I was not very pleased with Auntie Louie that night. When I got back to Roche, I 'told the tale', as we say, to mother. However, perhaps rightly, she was not sympathetic: "I think you should bear in mind, Kenneth,' she said, "that every one of Louie's boys is a shift-boss with The Company." The words 'The Company', spoken in the china clay area with a sort of oral genuflexion in the voice means English China Clays, the pre-dominant firm.

'Every one of Louie's boys is a shift-boss'. The proper Cornish (though not dialect) expression to use after such a statement is the single word 'Credit'. I have heard this many times. Auntie Louie had earned credit! It must have taken all her Hawken powers of contrivance and hard work; money must have been a constant problem. I can just remember – I must have been about six years old – that she came up to our house weeping. Some of the boys had no shoes; I lost a pair of wellingtons and a pair of shoes that morning. To my complaint that she was giving away my things, mother said we could get some more. The shop was beginning to do quite well.

Auntie Ella was my mother's youngest sister, and the one she was most close to. We usually went for a day's outing to Newquay on August Bank Holiday with her daughters Monica and Pamela, and with their father, Uncle Wes(ley), who eventually became a clay cap'n and was ordered, rather to his disgust, to wear a collar and tie. A favourite game was to pretend to be visitors. Monica was to be called Imogen (we had all read Enid Blyton's *Sunny Stories*). I was Graham – I now think I could have done better with Miles or Giles or something similar. Monica, who like her mother was up to anything, would call out loudly: "I say, Graham, I've found a simply ducky little pool!" Reading John Betjeman, who might well have been staying at Daymer Bay, near Padstow, just at this time, I am surprised how well we did. Betjeman has one upper-class visitor to Cornwall say: 'Prue! Primsie! Mumsie wants you. Sleepibyes'.

Auntie Ella, from the time when she reached the age of puberty (and I imagine well before) had a compulsion for matchmaking second only to Mrs Bennet in Jane Austen's *Pride and Prejudice*. She saw every young person in terms of marital prospects. Such and such a girl was 'some good maid to work'; a rather nondescript man was 'a lovely little fella'. There might of course be drawbacks: a young man she knew was 'bravish looking but awful smutty-mouthed' – (mouthed having two syllables.) She was helped by Cornish proverbs on matters of courtship, as when a man goes courting a distant partner: 'The lane id'n longer than the love'; or the cautionary 'Cousins do breed idiots'. And there is the general rule: 'Man's place to try, woman's to deny'.

My mother's youngest sister had plenty of spirit. One day she had a fancy for a bunch of lily of the valley, and posting mother outside the gate of a recently vacated house to mount guard, she crawled in to the garden on her belly to pick a sizeable bunch. However, in spite of her vitality and zest for life she did not live to a great age; she had had rheumatic fever in childhood and she did not have the strong heart of the other Hawkens; she died in middle age.

I have recently been in correspondence with Auntie Ella's daughter, my cousin Monica. She now lives in Huddersfield, because in 1944 just before D-Day a Yorkshire military policeman came courting her with his Alsatian. By telepathy or osmosis, or something, Monica and I find we are both engaged on the same theme – writing about Roche in the forties. She as an Anglican writes from a different viewpoint, for a Huddersfield parish magazine. Like me she has evolved a suitable style for this sort of thing: plain, sensible English. In this we have both avoided the method we were both taught by Mr Lean in Roche School; this was what he called 'cream English'. He would say, "'Monica ran down the road' is not as good as 'Sturdy little Monica went bounding down the road' ". Neither Monica nor I seem to agree with him, and I am sure we are right.

Monica adds a note for me on the Hawken choice of names. Grandma Hawken had wanted her youngest child to be called Monica; but this name was delayed a generation because Granda Hawken, on the way to the Registry Office, decided he could not spell it; but he happened to meet someone called Ella, and that solved his problem.

However, the name Monica was eventually given by Auntie Ella to her own daughter. But what about a second name? It was one of those occasions when I hope I 'turn after' my mother. There was a 'lovely shawl' on sale in Roche Co-op where mother worked. She did not have much money to spare, for certain; but as we Cornish say, 'they could have her heart'. If they would call the baby Monica Lilian, mother would buy her the shawl. I am sure mother had never read Wordsworth, but she would have agreed with his dictum: 'Give all thou canst:/ High heaven rejects the lore/ Of nicely calculated loss or more'.

Uncle Wes and Auntie Ella would sometimes come for supper after chapel and church on Sunday evenings. Father and Uncle Wes would take in turns 'telling the tale'; and at times the tales might be rather lewd, and in broad dialect such as you would not hear today. (It is an appalling fact that very few Cornish dialect stories are currently in print). Then Auntie Ella would get up with a twinkle in her eye that showed she had appreciated the proceedings; "Come on, Wes; 'tis time we went home". She would thump him gently on the arm: "Nobody would think you was a clay cap'n!"

She was, of course, immensely proud of him.

It is not surprising, in big families, that some children 'turn after' the father, others after the mother. Auntie Ella was not a Hawken, with their thin lips, but a Bate, her mother's family, with their prominent eyes. These were still more pronounced in her brother, Uncle Fred, of whose eyes father once said, "You could knock them off with a knitting needle." Poor Uncle Fred had more than his share of troubles; he was early a widower, his daughter was killed in a car crash while still a teenager, and his son died of a heart attack in early middle age. When asked what dialect word we could least spare, I always say *wisht* (melancholy) remembering the consolation given to Uncle Fred about his daughter by the saintly Canon Gilbert of St. Stephens: "You must remember, Mr Hawken, that heaven would be a wisht place if 'twas only old people there."

When I wrote some articles in *The Western Morning News* in which I gave, so my father's family thought, too much credit to the Hawkens, I was called to account by the Phillippses: "You ought to realise, Kenneth, that it is the Phillippses who have the brains; nobody goes for brains to the Hawkens."

I have thought about this a good deal. It is true that the Phillippses, not now a large family, have had their share of trophies: an Oxford D.Phil., a Bard of the Gorsedd, a county councillor, a headmistress, a headmaster. Strongly professional, they have freed themselves from the stigma (so far as there is one) of 'trade'. The Hawkens are less 'professional', I suppose; but they had a clay cap'n and NCO's of the claywork in the shape of shift-bosses, and a deputy headmistresss who, sadly, died young. The Huddersfield descendants of the Hawken family have also done well as teachers. They have people of practical ability such as electricians and talented amateur confectioners. And they had Uncle Will.

I have kept the best wine until last. Uncle Will had the Hawken constitution, and great powers of 'lowster' (hard work). He lived to be over eighty, rearing a big family. His only education would have been Roche elementary school yet by 1916, in his early twenties, he was accomplished enough to write very funny dialect stories like 'A Cheap Pig' for Netherton's *Cornish Almanack*. At fourteen he would have gone, like many others, as a kettle-boy making tea and warming pasties in the 'cuddy'. The big break would come when he no longer did this easy work but took to the lowster of the pick and shovel. I once saw a television programme that dealt partly with this transition. The narrator told how he would return as a youth from the unaccustomed labour at the claypit, aching all over. His mother massaged and rubbed his back, and the speaker's comment, with arms outspread in a pulpit gesture, was "True maternal affection, my friends!"

To test Will's stamina someone, a clay captain probably, said to the young man, "Will, how fast can 'ee dig up that piece of burden?" A bystander commented, "He went up through there like a want" (mole). What I remember most is his ability to set the back seat of a coach party laughing. We might pass, on Dartmoor in August, some farmers still carrying hay. Uncle Will's comment was; "A few miles and they'll be skating dressing" (spreading dung), normally a February activity. Of a chapel steward who pawed the air as he walked: "Living confirmation of Darwin", he said. When a Darby and Joan outing took place he started counting the passengers as they left the coach; "Yes, I thought so. Several more than when we set out. Some born on the way!"

No doubt it was his industry that led to his being selected by Cap'n Jack Goldsworthy for a special breakdown gang at Wheal Prosper, a claywork in Roche parish. Not so predictable was that he wrote, and published, dialect verse about the gang. Alongside his wit there had always been poetry: 'Poetry maketh a witty man', said Francis Bacon.

The family might not have agreed. This dialect verse was, to them, 'Will's nonsense'. An example might be a short poem he wrote in his youth on the death of a donkey (or 'dunkey', as we say):

> Here lies poor John Hammer's dunkey,
> Years he had about two score;
> He did die upon a Monday,
> Boys will serve him rough no more.

This plangent last line is, of course, dialect: *serve him right* is English; *serve him bad* or *serve him rough* is Cornish dialect.

For some years now I have adjudicated the Gorsedd dialect verse competition. There are good entries, but a great deal of faulty rhyme, rhythm and scansion. Uncle Will would not have written these. I remember being at a Bude Gorsedd many years ago and seeing him go up to receive yet another prize for verse. When his name was called he had a very rapid comb of his hair before going up. This was typical; his nickname was Shiner, which in dialect means a dandy, a dressy man. In 1974 when he was eighty the family clubbed together and a slim, limited edition of *Shiner's Poems* was produced by an Oxford publisher. They were all, of course, in careful and very authentic Cornish dialect and equally careful verse.

Of the Hawkens of that generation that I knew only Lilian, my mother is left for me to describe. She was older than Auntie Ella but younger than Auntie Louie. She had the Hawken gift of being able to fit in with others. She often used to talk about the lively times they had when she worked at the Co-op. It will be a sad day when humour arises only from secondhand sources, from sitcom and videoed comedy and not from real-life situations. Real-life comedy would be constantly recalled, leading to the slow maturing of old jokes: "Here, do 'ee mind the time when . . ." and so on. Mother loved to tell of a 'green' new shop assistant who was given such strict and detailed instructions about not breaking a very special oil-jar that she managed to do just that as she delivered it. "They used to pull her leg shocking", said mother.

Mother was much shrewder than this, but at times she could be not so much naive as flamboyantly ignorant – the fine flowering of ignorance, as Oscar Wilde says somewhere. One of her best efforts in this line was her reply to the proud father of a successful cricketer; "Robin took four wickets for twenty runs!" Mother's comment was "Never mind!"

"Oh, but it's good," said the father, taken aback.

"I don't think I said the right thing there, Kenneth. But then I don't study cricket," mother confessed later.

"Yes you did, mother," I said. "You couldn't have done better."

But she did do better, as those who know the Cornish dialect will appreciate. The word *ta*, an unrecorded but not uncommon nursery word, means to defecate, to 'do number two' in hospital parlance. I remember the Roche infant teacher conferring with an underling: "We don't say that word, do we Miss Brown? We say 'May we leave the room', not 'Go to ta'" But mother had misheard a phrase that caused her some perplexity, especially as it was broadcast on the national news: 'A two-day ta; that must have been terrible", she said. And yet I cannot think of a better comment on a *coup d'etat*. In 1968, when General de Gaulle returned to Paris to quell student rebellion his comment was "Reforme, oui; mais pas un chie-en-lit". It is the same idea.

Mother was no antiquarian. Later in life, if we decided to go out in the car, she would give definite directions: "Nowhere historical, eh? Somewhere where there's nice shops." In fact shops, for mother, were the great attraction of the towns. A friend's father used to drive out to the Roche area to pick mushrooms. This she found incomprehensible. "Whatever do Mr Woodhouse come out here picking mushrooms for? You can get lovely tinned stuff in St. Austell."

Modernity was the thing, so far as mother was concerned. I have heard her say many times "'Tis so well to be out of the world as out of the fashion." But one or two modern things defeated her. "'Tis no good, Doreen" she said sadly to my sister, "I shall never like they hambuggers!"

This string of anecdotes may suggest that mother was a figure of fun. That would be wrong. Though not very knowledgeable she was wise. I once won a *Spectator* competition about pollution by focussing on the china clay industry. Mother was very angry: "I don't know about the Phillippses," she said, "but we Hawkens would be nowhere without the clay. 'Tis no good to get biggotty while you've still got to earn your living." In all disputes between the family and outsiders she was, as the Cornishman is alleged to have said about the Pope, 'a tiger to fight'. Since her one indulgence was liquorice allsorts, sacrifice came easily to her. Many times during the war I heard her say, "'Twill do the children more good than 'twill we."

Her faith was never far from her mind; and she was, as the Methodist Sunday School hymnbook expresses it, 'not ashamed to own her Lord'. Another wartime memory is of her comment when news came over the wireless 'casualties were heavy' or 'three of our aircraft are missing'. It was as if from a Methodist litany that she would repeat: "'Tis somebody's every time".

She was never as keen on making money as father was. "Come out and see this handsome sunset," she would say on a fine summer evening. He always came out to see.

Father exploited to the full her Hawken capacity for hard work. By the late thirties all the better-off woman had their hair permed; and mother aspired to join their ranks. She staged a small rebellion in which she said that she was doing two jobs: housekeeping and shopkeeping. Father said, "Nothing is nicer than bobbed hair," but she got her perm, and I at least was pleased; though privately I thought that the zig-zag perms of the thirties were not very beautiful.

Mother rightly took it as a compliment, though not everybody would, when a saleswoman in a Truro shop told her, as she was buying some gloves for a wedding: "My dear, I can see by the

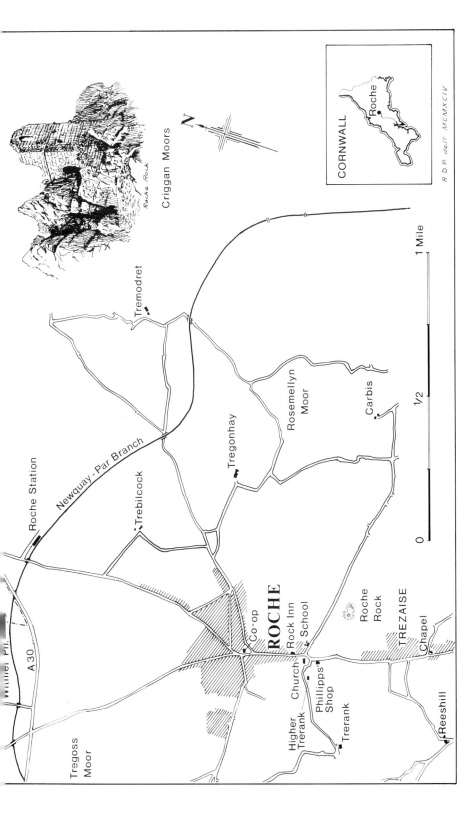

CORNWALL

Roche

R D P delt MCMXCIV

Criggan Moors

Roche Rock

N

Tremodret

Roche Station

Newquay - Par Branch

Trebilcock

Tregonhay

Rosemellyn Moor

Carbis

A 30

Tregoss Moor

Co-op

ROCHE

Rock Inn

School

Church

Phillipps' Shop

Roche Rock

TREZAISE

Chapel

Higher Trerank

Trerank

Reeshill

0   ½   1 Mile

Some of the Phillipps Family

Great grandfather Job and his wife Charlotte

Granda Phillipps

*Top: Edith and Frank
Middle: Charlie
Lower: Alice and David*

Some of the Hawken Family

The Kendall family with Granda Hawken

Uncle Will out Rock

Uncle Charlie Roberts and Auntie Louie

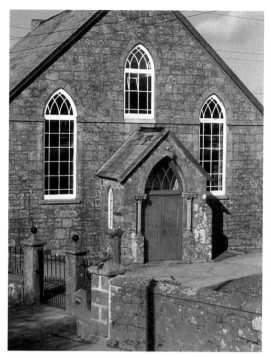

Trezaise Chapel

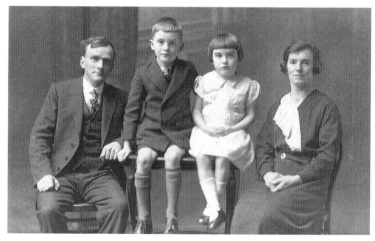

Phillipps family in 1937

Three Roche Teachers

Mr Lean

Mr Harvey

Mrs Tabb

The Shop

The Shopkeepers

A Cousin in Every Chapel

*Mrs Ruby Hugo
at Gunwen*

*Mrs Grace Tippett at
Greensplat*

Roche Rock

'If heaven is like Withel as perhaps it may be'

colour of your hands that you've worked hard all your life, as I've had to do." Yet mother had her consolations. Like her brothers and sisters she was totally at home in the classless society of her childhood. She loved recalling that one evening at a village social she won a raffle, and everyone burst into loud applause. "And," she would say, "if I was short of a bed for the night, at least a dozen homes would put me up".

But it would not be true to say that she had absolutely no dealings with the great. Father had a good deal to do with the Young Farmers and mother accompanied him to rallies at Pencarrow and elsewhere. One of the high points of her existence was when Sir John Molesworth St. Aubyn came over to her and shook hands, as he did more than once:

'Good morning, Mrs Phillipps."
'Good morning, Sir John."

I don't suppose the late lord of Pencarrow knew how much pleasure he was conferring; but I think the situation might apply with many of the Cornish gentry. Townees may sneer; but that is why they are townees.

Chapter 4

Comin' On

Delightful task! To rear the tender thought. To teach the young idea how to shoot.

Having left school a few years my father took the only examination he ever sat for (I suspect he would have liked more; whereas I had a normal dislike of exams). This was an exam in shoeing horses, in 1921; and the family still have the framed certificate of the Worshipful Company of Farriers (The Princess Royal is also a Fellow). There is a superstition that loose horse-shoes should be depicted, and also hung, with the round part at the bottom to prevent the luck running out at the two ends. But the Worshipful Company of Farriers waives this rule, and the two brawny farriers drawn on the Certificate of Fellowship are surrounded by horse-shoes with ends pointing downwards.

When his old blacksmith's shop in the middle of Roche Hill was badly damaged by a fire in the next-door carpenter's shop, granda, with admirable foresight built, in 1923, a really capacious black-smith's shop of three large rooms. It included a sort of big bay window for displaying goods. Young Charlie must have considered his prospects, particularly since horses were used less and the farm machines that replaced them were factory-made. At Easter 1924 he opened an ironmonger's shop in one of the three rooms: "If I'd opened in January," he told me, "I should have given up". January, too early for spring cleaning, was a bad time for ironmongery.

Meanwhile the friendship with Lilian Hawken continued, though there was little prospect of marriage. Mother saved with something called the Blanket Club; father in National Savings. Like all employees of the Co-op, mother could be at the mercy of the committee of voluntary inspectors, all Co-op committee members anxious to assert what little authority they had. So when in the evening she dressed Charlie's window with ironmongery, they drew the blind first.

Several times I have heard them repeat an odd little courtship ritual:

> Good evening miss.
> Good evening.
> Taking company, miss?
> Not your sort, thank you.

They both followed the old Methodist custom, that was to be found also in Wales, of continuing at Sunday School till they married, sometimes as pupils, sometimes as teachers. In the mean time the Hawken family had moved from Riverside on the Fal, to Roche Council Houses – 'out Council', as it was called. From here the younger generation were married; they had no desire for the single life. It was a lively household; they invested in a wind-up gramophone and played songs like 'The Laughing Policeman', or 'Felix kept on walking, kept on walking still!' or 'Ain't it grand to be blooming well dead'.

Eventually in 1928, Lilian and Charlie married. She was not in white but in a grey 'costoom'. The wedding took place, like most Phillipps weddings, in Zion Chapel, St. Austell. The honeymoon was in Exeter; and on the Sunday morning they attended that Mecca of Westcountry Methodism, the Mint Chapel, Exeter.

There was no employment for married women in those days, and it was quite a come-down from the wage of nearly £2 a week that mother had been earning from the Co-op to the combined profits of blacksmithing and ironmongery, not more than about 30/- to support them both. In ten months (just in time!) a scraggy baby boy made his appearance. There are four phrases to describe ill-favoured children and people in the Cornish dialect; and mother eventually used all of them of me: I was 'behind the door when good looks was gived out'; I had a 'face like a diseased boot'; I had 'a good face for a ugly jug' (Toby jug); or 'a face like a child's ass after nine days' slapping'. When told at the birth that it was a boy, not the hoped-for girl, she said, "Well, I suppose I shall get to lov'n". But eventually she took up a different position: "Of course, I serve the children both alike; but I shan't see the boy put down".

My earliest memories come from occasions like the putting in of piped water in our terrace house in Trezaise Road. I echoed the neighbour's cry of "Oo, look, the tap is skitting" (splashing). By twelve months, so I have been told, I had quite a good vocabulary, though I was slower at walking; and that is enough to convict me of mendacity; for as the Cornish proverb goes, 'If a chield can talk before it can walk, 'tis goin' to be a liard'. Ability to walk eventually arrived, suddenly. While mother was listing my accomplishments to a friend I called out: "Yes, and I can walk by myself. Look!" It must have been the spirit of Auntie Ethel. But the mixture of a sense of drama with showing-off is very characteristic of me.

As to vocabulary, some of my earliest words were made-up: for example *jang-jang* for one of those metal-cased flat torches with bulbous heads and noisy switches – you never see them now – and *seven-eight* for an abacus.

At the age of about four I walked into granda's blacksmith's shop and casually picked up a piece of iron from the anvil. It was only just not red-hot, and the pain was acute. Auntie Hannah administered gauze and bandage, and I sobbed bitterly, "No little boy had to suffer like I have had to suffer" – thus early revealing my besetting sin of self-pity.

At about this time I got into trouble for mischievously mixing 'kibbled maize' (chopped maize for the fowls) with turpentine. This was in Higher Terank where the maize was kept in an open chimney, behind a curtain. Formerly there had been a 'cloam oven' here, as was also indicated by the bellying out of the outside wall. Grandma was incensed at what I had done and called me a Turk; something I greatly resented: "She needn't have called me a Turk!" I complained. I did not know then why the Turks represented for grandma the epitome of all wickedness. But she would have been a girl going to Bugle school and from a Liberal household in 1877 when she would have read or heard read, in *The Western Morning News* perhaps, of the Bulgarian atrocities. Mr Gladstone said on that occasion "that the Turks, one and all, bag and baggage, shall I hope clear out from the province they have desolated and profaned."

Doreen, my sister, two years younger than me, attended school for the first time in 1935. I remember the date, because I was beginning to be aware of my position in the infant school. On the afternoon of her first day I was designated Sukey, and my task was to take off the kettle from the Tortoise stove in the schoolroom:

> Sukey take it off again,
> They've all gone away.

But Doreen, seeing me as I suppose she might, in difficulties, jumped up and ran out to help: "Kenneth, take your little sister into the cloakroom and clean her up." I can still remember the green jumper, smutted from the kettle, and how she reacted to my black looks.

A few years later Doreen was very ill with pneumonia and pleurisy. I was shipped off to stay with Auntie Edith, to return to see the patient a week later, when she appeared very ill indeed. No doubt antibiotics would accomplish much now; but at that time she had to have a fire in her room, and wore a poultice, which gradually diminished, around her middle. The doctor visited for months and told mother she must thank God it was not tubercular. For myself, I was glad to escape from the sickroom and to help Uncle Owen with the rabbits.

But the following June I realised for the first, but by no means the last time that I was very lucky to have been born in Roche. Doreen was still in bed most of the time. She was constantly being sent presents from well-wishers in the village. When the band for the Feast procession passed our house, it stopped and played special music. There seemed to be a collective will for her to get better; she got better.

For a while Doreen peaked and pined; but eventually was fully recovered and in due course went on to County School in St. Austell. She began to look forward to leaving school. My headmaster at St. Austell Boys' School met her socially and liked her, but he told me she should have more drive. All headmasters talk like this, as if we should all be Lucifers, maximising our ambition. My sister is a natural villager. I feel that since her ancestors have lived in Roche for at least four centuries she might well love the place. There is another viewpoint of course; this was put by another Roche native, Mrs Ruskin Spear: "I spent too many holidays out Roche Rock".

Doreen tended to take her friends from the Hawken side of the family: 'All the Phillippses do give 'ee is superfluous hairs', she said. She subsidised the cosmetics industry. I remember she sent me to St. Austell on an errand – for blustery weather lotion. The assistant had never heard of it. What was it for? Adopting the slightly bemused tone of a supercilious male I said, 'Blustery weather'. The assistant managed to find a bottle. Doreen generally got what she wanted.

Despite quite a bit of illness, my sister has inherited and retained her father's sense of humour. She once developed symptoms of a grumbling appendix, when a certain Mrs Cap'n Tremayne made the sympathetic comment: "A grumbling appendix! And 'tis fatil, idn it!" Doreen was greatly comforted!

Mrs Captain Tremayne of course, had been married to a clay captain and retained the title, though a widow. This was Roche etiquette! Mother never forgot to include 'Cap'n' on the grounds that many are called 'Mrs', but few are chosen clay cap'ns' wives.

As she moved about the house mother would sing 'snatches of old songs'. She would have started school in 1905 or 1906; and by this time ballads of the older English type were probably being recognised and recommended; songs like *Cruel Barbara Allen*, which in spite of its glorious tune I found morbid in sentiment, at least when I was five. Later, I recognised the authentic, aggrieved accents of village gossip in the words:

> And all she said, when there she came,
> Young man, I think you're dying.

That would be called in Roche 'a burnen' shame'. But more to my taste was that lively, bubbly tune, *Jockey to the Fair*; this was the tune that Gabriel Oak, in Hardy's *Far from the Madding Crowd*, continued to play on the flute after the ruin of his fortunes. I do not know why this fine tune never seems to be broadcast; but perhaps we should be thankful that Benjamin Britten did not lay hands on it, tarnishing the major key and clear harmonies. As mother sang it around the kitchen there was no hint of such things.

As she sang in the evenings when doing the ironing, mother would accompany herself with the sounds of the old box iron (there was no electricity). At the age of about five, as I lay in bed upstairs, the click-click of the red-hot iron in its box seemed to me the most soothing rhythm in the world.

In his *The History of Mr Polly*, published in 1910, H.G.Wells detects a less worthy strand in the songs of his day. As he puts it, Mr Polly and his friends 'would have sung catches if they had known how to do it; but as it was they sang melancholy music-hall songs about dying soldiers and the old folks far away.'

Most of the songs that mother sang were of this kind. Some were from a book of popular songs that her father acquired from his sailor brother. Granda Hawken would sing them with his children in Reeshill as they lay in bed together late on a Sunday morning. These songs as I recall them are really 'snatches' – this one, I imagine, must be about Ireland:

And the tears rolled down his sunburnt cheeks,
And dropped on the letter in his hand,
" 'Tis true, too true,
More trouble in my native land."

This one is a Victorian charity outing:

From near and far, the children come,
From court and alley, lane and slum,
To spend a bright and happy day
Which far too soon will pass away.

Emotion was not held back in these songs, especially on the
theme of mother-love:

She kissed me and she called me her darling,
Around me her arms she did throw.
I shall never forget that sad parting,
When I said, 'Mother, dear, I must go'.

Or the better-known:

Then cherish her with care
And smooth her silver hair,
When gone, you will never have another.
For, wherever you may turn
This lesson you may learn:
A boy's best friend is his mother.

'This lesson you may learn' – this didactic element in poetry and
song is now by no means so evident as it was in Victorian times.
Mother's favourite poem, learnt at school, no doubt, is saturated
with counsel:

Waste not, want not, this maxim I would teach,
Let your watchword be 'never despair' and practise
  what you preach.
Never let your chances like sunbeams pass you by,
For you'll never miss the water till the well runs dry.

When I was six father bought a brand new Philips piano in a
bankruptcy sale. Uncle David said it was a white elephant. But
soon I was going to Mrs S.C.Tabb (born a Trethewey). After her

name were the letters A.T.C.L. – Associate of Trinity College, London. More important than her letters, Mrs Tabb could teach very effectively. I have known more glorious letters which were the property of people who couldn't teach anybody anything. But then, I don't suppose Mrs Tabb ever read a book on educational theory in her life; that may well account for why she was so effective. I went for lessons on Tuesday afternoons; and early on Tuesday evenings Sam, Mrs Tabb's husband, used to have fish-cakes for his tea. So the lesson might be interrupted by brief visits to the kitchen.

But it didn't matter. Soon I was practising not only scales (I did not like scales much) but hymn tunes from the Methodist Sunday School tune book, and thus taking my turn at accompanying the Sunday School services. You gather that nobody was allowed in Trezaise to bury their talents; in fact the parable of the talents was rammed home: not to practise meant not to have; not to use was not to be able. Once, as she was dusting the piano keys before a lesson Mrs Tabb gave me a sudden clip on the ear with the duster. I was so taken aback that it cured my hiccups instantly!

My talent for singing had been spotted by Miss Richards in the infant school; and I was put to sing, at the age of six, when one of the school governors visited. This would be Mrs Stanley Marshall, the mother of Roche's only knight, Sir Archie Marshall, the presiding judge at the Stephen Ward trial, connected with the Profumo affair in 1963.

As a boy soprano, notably at the Indian Queens music festival and at St. Austell, I was a regular performer. The adjudicator at Queens was often a man called Thomas F.Dunhill who had written some of the test pieces. He would sit there as the competitors came forward in order, as on the programme. It required nerve to stand on the platform until the adjudicator had finished writing up the last contestant: 'attractive in tone; not quite true at the end'. Then, having finished writing, Thomas F.Dunhill would ring his little bell. It was your turn!

At the very first contest I went to at Queens I won, as a third prize, a bronze medal. When I brought it home in its little green box granda nearly jumped out of his chair. "Well", he said laconically, but it was enough! A year or two later I should hardly have deigned to pick up a third prize. But, as the octogenarian Mrs Tabb reminded me recently, at St. Austell at the age of seven I was so excited at having won first prize that I applauded myself. I wonder whether too much excitement so young is a good thing.

Mother had definite ideas about goals: "I want to be able to go

Market House in St. Austell and bring home any piece of music, and for you to put'n on the music-stand and rattle'n off''. Till I went to the grammar school, I was succeeding quite well in these aims; and even now, if my pension was stopped, I suppose I might earn some sort of a living in a pub; though the music I 'rattled off' would now be very old-fashioned. Moreover, I now play by ear and that is death to the improving of technique. But in any case mother's aims and mine were soon at variance because, sad to say, I developed a tendency to musical snobbery. After two or three years with Mrs Tabb I was playing 'characteristic pieces' as they were called, 'Lola' or 'Nola' and so on, and they were mildly syncopated. I plucked up courage and asked 'For my next piece could I try somebody really famous? Could I try Bach?'

Mrs Tabb was greatly surprised. Bach was all right of course. 'Jesu, joy of man's desiring' was a handsome piece. But lots of Bach, like preludes and fugues and stuff – they were 'dry as chips'.

I call this good honest Philistinism. Mrs Tabb on Bach is like George III on Shakespeare: 'Was there ever . . . such stuff as great part of Shakespeare? Only one mustn't say so.'

Mrs Tabb, meeting mother at a Faith Tea, commented that my piano playing had improved as a result of this new regime. It may be objected that with hindsight I am describing a precocity rather hoped for than real; but I vividly remember that I was being served a diet of Nolas, Lolas, 'Tiptoe through the tulips' and perhaps worst of all, Ketelby: 'In a Persian Market', 'In a Monastery Garden', 'In a Lithuanian Latrine' and so on.

I also fought a battle against having to sing rubbish. To father who was musically illiterate a song called 'Daddy' represented a summit of musical achievement:

> Lay your head on my shoulder, daddy,
> Turn your face to the west;
> It is just the hour that the skies turn gold,
> The hour that mother loved best.

I never sang this horrible song. ''That's the worst of Kenneth,'' said mother, ''He do always go for this highbrow stuff''. What I really liked at this time was Schubert's setting of the song from *Cymbeline*: 'Hark, hark the lark'.

But if I hoped for approval from the Trethewey élite for this song I was doomed, rightly, to disappointment. As Mrs Tabb and I practised it in the Sunday school, her father Charlie Thethewey sat absentmindedly twiddling the poker in the Tortoise stove.

When I had finished he asked:

"Whose music is that then, Muriel?"
"Schubert's, father."
"Oh, yes."

Being sent around the central Cornwall area as a soloist gave a good impression of the homogeneity of Methodism: in every chapel there was a classroom to house the artists before they emerged, a chairman to announce items on the programme, a doorkeeper or two to pick up the collection. In the early days there would be an organ blower. Some places were more lively than others. There was Greensplat, near Hensbarrow beacon and consequently the loftiest in situation of any Methodist chapel in the county, probably. Fifty-five years ago I went to perform at concerts in Greensplat. As became the more rarified air, perhaps, things were a little more frivolous there. "Purdy!" the audience would shout if the entertainment pleased them, "Purdy" and they would clap their hands and stamp their feet in approval (stamping of feet was frowned on in chapels below the tree-line). Afterwards there would be hot pasties and jelly served on the hymnbook ledges.

As early as September 1933 when I started at Roche infants' school I made my first friend. His name was Charlie Common and we have been friends for sixty years. He was a year older than me but started later because he lived farther from the school at Lower Trerank on the River Fal.

Soon, each Christmas, I would be going to Charlie's for a party. The Commons were hardworking smallholders; and the party would have to break off while Charlie's father brought in the milk and his mother strained it and washed the buckets. The filter pads for the strainers I have no doubt would have come from C.T. Phillipps.

The Christmas tea was always good; nothing 'boughten' because 'boughten stuff' had no goodness; and in any case 'twas expensive, 'aiten money'. There would be games like 'Mrs Mackenzie's very ill'. I don't know how this frail Scotswoman came to be so prevalent in Cornwall. As the game proceeds her symptoms become not only more severe but more life-threatening for the players. "Yes, she do scratch 'er head with 'er right hand and 'er nose with 'er left; pass it on." The usual phrase in Roche for death after a prolonged illness is a 'happy release'. Some considerate player achieves this by announcing: "Mrs Mackenzie's dead!" And gradually the room collapses into inactivity after violent contortions.

Once a week or so, winter and summer, Mrs Common would take a big basket, fill it with the produce of Lower Trerank, butter and eggs, and walk the mile and a half to Roche station. It would all be taken to Newquay to sell. With butter there would be some profit; but with eggs, she said "You don't see a new penny for an old one."

What did she go to all this trouble for? For Charlie, of course. Anybody with half an eye could see that Charlie was 'university material' as they say nowadays. But there was no guarantee of a scholarship or grant in the nineteen thirties. At home I felt the same pressures. As they say in dialect, "twas which and which' between Charlie and me. He was better at sums, I at 'composition'; eventually he got two science degrees. Many years later Mr Lean, the schoolmaster, told me it was very good to have two such clever boys and to promote friendly rivalry between them. Charlie and I never fell out; and one of the reasons was we went to the same chapel at Trezaise. Charlie to use a vernacular phrase 'would not come behind'. If Kenneth Phillipps had a piano Charlie must have one too; and because he practised his scales harder than me he overtook me in piano-playing and when we played duets I thumped away on the bass. For a long time now he has not been happy unless he has an organ to play or a choir to conduct.

My memories of childhood are sharp, and I particularly remember my first introduction to politics at the general election of 1935, when I was six. In the mid-Cornwall division there were three candidates: Mr Maurice Petherick (Tory), Mr A.L. Rowse (Labour) and a Liberal candidate who I thought was a Mr Percy Harris, but the reference books say different.

In 1935 I was in the infant school, which was ruled with a rod of iron, or rather with a stinging knitting-needle, by Miss Richards and her able assistant Miss Ward (still with us). A few days before the election a Mr Salter from big school came across, urging Miss Richards to vote Labour. The class was set to silent reading; but no way (to adopt a later idiom) no way was I going to carry on silent reading with this lot going on. I recall that Miss Richards was pale and tight-lipped as she repeated: "I stick to my guns, I stick to my guns, I will have nothing to do with that Mr Leslie Rowse. I have it on good authority that that young man is an atheist."

Atheist? What did that mean? I would ask mother when I got home. Mother's answer was direct: an atheist was someone who didn't believe in Jesus.

Well here, of course, I was right behind Miss Richards. We didn't want any of that.

Mr Salter went back to big school, crestfallen I supposed. But one of the great things about Roche in the old days was the existence of what librarians now call a good retrieval system. After seeing this row I wanted to know what happened next. And there was Mrs Balaam Hancock, the perfect retrieval system, ready to tell all. Mrs Balaam Hancock was the school caretaker, and very knowledgeable about things in general; and she said that Miss Richards and Miss Ward had painted a shield in the Labour colours with a golliwog on top – a golliwog because Mr Salter had frizzy hair. I was too young then to realise that they both rather liked Mr Salter in spite of all.

Polling day was a stream, in fact more than a stream, a millstream of rain, as we say; and those people that could afford it went to the polling booth in a taxi driven by Mr Marcus Trethewey.

As to the result, as I have seen happen many times since, the Conservative from being an apparent outsider came top of the poll. And Mr Leslie Rowse came second; and the Liberal was third. This last worried me; granda had taken me to that palatial Whig house, Lanhydrock; and he said that one of the trees in the park had been planted by Mr Gladstone. And grandma had a tea-caddy with a faded picture of Mr Gladstone on it. On such a basis a lifetime's political affiliations can be formed – indeed, have been formed. I applied to mother again.

"They there Liberals; do they believe in Jesus?"

"Sure to," said mother, "they there big Liberals is mostly chapel-going."

Political theory was mother's strong suit!

After the excitement of the election things carried on in a more humdrum way. Some time later, at Easter, Miss Richards as usual enacted the Crucifixion by leaning against a glass cupboard with a sad expression on her face and outstretched arms. This performance could reduce those of us who were tender-hearted to tears.

Years later – forty years later, and after she had spent some time in the County Asylum – someone showed Miss Richards a copy of an article I had written in *The Western Morning News*.

"It's by Kenneth Phillipps," she said. "Yes, I remember Kenneth. I could make him cry".

One day in the infant school a former headmaster, Mr Dempster, came into the classroom, holding behind his back a squeaker which squeaked noisily. Mr Dempster then held it up and asked the question "What is a workhouse?" I put up my hand – I liked squeakers – and said, "It is a place where poor people live".

"Who is that boy? Is that Charles's boy?" (He had taught father at the beginning of the century.)

The squeaker is practically the only inheritance I had via my father.

The subject taught badly in most schools nowadays (if it is taught at all) is R.E., or Scripture as we used to call it. Even when I was a pupil in Roche 'big school' it was badly done; the time allocated was mostly given up to a wartime effort to collect National Savings. However, while we were in the infant school, scripture was business. Like so many of the Methodists I have known Miss Richards had a strong sense of drama. She made up her own script; but her authority was unquestioned. She would pick up the five slingstones from the brook for the imaginary David; and then have him standing up to the fierce Goliath. How his words would ring out from Miss Richards's lips: "You come to me with a sword; and with a spear and with a shield; but I come to you in the name of the Lord."

We were called upon (rightly, I suppose) to approve of Miriam's crafty ruse in getting her mother to look after (OT 'nurse') brother Moses. I also remember still the minatory tones in which Miss Richards (as the Angel of the Lord) called out "Abraham, Abraham, don't you touch Isaac!" Fortunately, you may recall, there was a ram for Abraham's sacrificial use caught by the horns in a thicket, Miss Richards laid her hair against the partition between the classrooms in a not very successful attempt at rendering this.

It is a curious fact that I remember no lessons so well as I remember Miss Richards's scripture lessons. She led me astray only once; I am ashamed to say how old I was when I learnt what really happened between Joseph and Potiphar's wife. According to Miss Richards (and her writ ran so deep that I believed it for a long time) it was not adultery that Joseph was accused of: it was that he had been 'set up' as they say nowadays, and had been accused of theft.

In what must have been one of my more daring moments, I confided to Miss Richards, "Miss, my mammy said I got a head like a turnip!" "You tell your mummy, Kenneth, a turnip hasn't got brains." I repeated this story in Higher Trerank, to immense acclaim. People do not use the simple word 'brains' so much now, but talk of 'ability' and 'high IQ' etc. But the Phillippses knew what they meant. Kind hearts are more than coronets; money is always useful; but brains are a constant good, lasting to senility and beyond. My grandfather, uncle and aunts liked the phrase and repeated it: 'A turnip hasn't got brains'.

In the second volume of her autobiography, *Cornish Years*, Anne Treneer mentions visiting in Roche her friend Mrs Marjorie Harvey, nee Marjorie Pascoe, wife of the headmaster of Roche school, Harold Harvey. Anne Treneer wrote, 'I went to stay with the Harveys in the new white schoolhouse which was built for them near the hermitage of the Rock'. It was, I believe, owing to Marjorie Pascoe's father, F.R.Pascoe – Director of Education, in Truro – that the house was built; *Chy an Garek*, as it was called, the house near the Rock. I was a pupil in the last few years of Mr Harvey's reign, before he was dismissed. I have often thought that he reached his prime in the wrong decade. He would have done well in the more frivolous sixties, rather than the earnest thirties. He was a man of a hundred hobbies, and taught everything except the syllabus:[1] meteorology, handicraft, drama. His sports days were nothing if not innovative, one big item being what one might call a sort of land water-skiing. Triangular frames, built at the school, were ridden by a small boy and pulled by bigger ones. The frames were painted in the house colours of Tregarrick, Tremodrett, Trenoweth and Tregothnan – the first three being names of local farms. The less academic boys helped him to build a bell-tower for the school bell. Most important of all, as far as I was concerned, was the school concert each Christmas; always so-called, though in fact it was more like a pantomime. In 1937 I was chosen to play the name part in *Rumpelstiltskin*, and Mr Harvey had called me over to the school house, and had written two songs for me, trying out on the piano different tune endings: "Hm . . . no good, too much like a hymn". (Mr Harvey did not like hymns.) Perhaps it was just about this time that the fatal dismissal from Truro came. All rehearsals stopped. I should never again sing solos in the rather bare rooms of Chy an Garek.

There are no longer many who were old pupils of Mr Harvey; but they still attest great loyalty to him. They do not mind, as many of the Methodists did, that prayers were said about twice a week, and not, as according to regulations, twice a day. These survivors

---

[1] Much of this account was broadcast from Roche by Radio Cornwall at a special meeting of old scholars; and Mr Arnold Best warmly denied this statement, and asserted that Mr Harvey did keep to the syllabus. Mr Best has always been worth listening to, especially when he was the leading bass singer in mid-Cornwall; and it is very sad indeed that since October 1993 he is no longer with us.

still recall the concerts, and such events as the public folk-dancing, when Mr Harvey, wearing a mask, accompanied very expertly on a viola.

In June 1984, on the occasion of his death, he received a telling tribute. Nearly a dozen of his old pupils, then in their late fifties and sixties, went to Penmount for his cremation and asked permission to form a guard of honour. For those who have eyes to see, this was a far more moving farewell than many more formal tributes.

Mr Lean, who came as the new headmaster the following January, was very different. He began by shouting the assembled school into terrified silence on the first day; "This is what will happen because I say so – I say so." Discipline became noticeably stricter. Mr Harvey rarely resorted to corporal punishment; Mr Lean did fairly systematically. He rarely stopped caning until the culprit was in tears.

In one respect only did Mr Lean fail, judged by the standards of County Hall: he did not succeed in making all the boys wear neckties. Roche is a large village with extensive 'backwoods'; boys from the backwoods would not wear ties!

Mr Lean had two sons, the elder of whom, Bryn, became a friend of mine. He was as adept at all games as I was inept; and it was not long before out of the goodness of his heart he began centring balls in the playground for me to score a goal: "for," said he, "'tis terrible to have got to your age and not to have scored a single goal". In the end a goal was scored. "Hard work that was, Charlie," Bryn said. (He called me 'Charlie' in the Cornish patronymic way; I doubt if that would happen now.)[1] He and I moved to grammar school at the same time, but somehow we ceased to be very friendly, owing to my cantankerousness, and I regret this. Still, I made amends in the senior part of the school, where I translated most of the Latin, Virgil and Tacitus, supposed to be a joint effort. Perhaps he was not much better at Tacitus than I was at scoring goals.

The year after Mr Lean arrived war was declared, in 1939. Two days before the war broke out, as it happened, some of the Phillipps family had a trip in a taxi (an unheard of luxury, provided by the gentry) to Tredethy House, the home of the Hext family in

---

[1] My friend Squadron-Leader Lambert Dive, son of yet another Charlie, told me that in Padstow school playgrounds he was usually 'Charlie', not 'Lambert'; but he agrees with me that this patronymic tendency has died out.

the village of Helland on the edge of the Bodmin Moors. I think the treat must really have been Auntie Kathleen's; she had worked up to being not merely the housekeeper but a sort of unofficial financial adviser to the increasingly vague Miss Nellie Horndon, close relative of the Hexts. Miss Nellie was staying at Tredethy at this time.

A visit to a country-house, even a small one like Tredethy, before the National Trust was fully organised, was felt as a privilege. I can still remember details of that afternoon, curtailed though it was by the fact that the taxi had to be back at St. Austell station in time to meet evacuees. I remember the Hext family portraits in the main hall, including one of a boy in an eighteenth century coat of yellow; he was struggling with a difficult sum in a sum-book. There was a whole landing full of Haute École pictures of the Spanish Riding School – the family had been horse-mad.

The grounds of Tredethy were not extensive, but they contained a large mulberry tree; and many other trees arched over to form a sort of makeshift dance-hall, where the Wadebridge Conservatives used sometimes to hold a dance. We all had our tea sitting round the dining-room table; a rare example of the gentry copying the working-class; for I supposed they normally sat separately on chairs and ate cucumber sandwiches for their tea! But we sat at table (the event was called a tea-party) and ate sponge fingers; there was a spirit-lamp to keep the kettle warm.

But by this time the evacuees would have arrived, doubling the population of Roche, just as in 1944, before D-day, American soldiers were to quadruple it. The textbook version of the cheerful Cockney sparrow did not apply to these refugees from the 'phoney' war. The children were a dispirited, undernourished lot from Finsbury; somewhat inclined to bed-wetting. One of the teachers explained to Auntie Hannah: "They have no stamina". Nowadays, no doubt, more would be done to make the stranger welcome, but in 1939 there was only the chapel, offering alien concepts like thrift and teetotalism. Some young mothers with babies were especially inclined to have what T.S.Eliot calls 'damp souls'. They would wander about the four or five streets of downtown St. Austell, complaining bitterly of the boredom of village life, and before long they would be back in London, to return again when the blitz became severe.

A brighter picture of young London motherhood at this time was offered to us, many years later, by Mrs Margaret Parkyn, describing the emergency of evacuation in her native Mawgan-in-Pydar. This favoured place was clearly more suitable than Roche for mothers with small babies. However, there was a crisis; and a bustling organiser referred to by Mrs Parkyn as 'Marge', sent out a red alert, an appeal for thirty-two small chamber-pots for thirty-two mothers with toddlers. So dire was the need that the appeal was soon answered, and at a special meeting in the village hall, the venture was seen by Marge as a matter for congratulation. Mothers, babies and pots were all assembled.

But as ill luck would have it, someone accidentally pushed one chamber-pot off a chair.

A hoarse voice whispered (we shall never know; it could well have been Mrs Parkyn) "Marge haven't got but thirty-one now!"

This anecdote of 1939 Mrs Parkyn told me in the seventies. Pat, my father and I went to Mawgan to meet her, and she showed us round her lovely village, so different from the blowsiness of nearby Newquay. She clearly remembered the novelist, Charles Lee, who had lived here for a time and had played the organ in the village church. I did not know then that I should have the luck to be able to buy Lee's Journal. She showed us the site of the shop once kept by two Mawgan spinsters and described in his short story, 'The White Bonnet' (*Our Little Town*). For me, to read about this untidy shop was to be reminded of our shop in Roche. Mrs Parkyn was a keen member of the British Legion; and also, as frequently happens in the village of Mawgan with its convent, a devout Catholic. She showed us around Lanherne, originally home of the Arundell family, and where, it is said, the sanctuary lamp has not gone out since the Reformation.

As we passed the holy water stoup Mrs Parkyn reached in with her fingers and 'skit' (splashed) father. "There you are, you old Methodist", she said, "you *shall* have some holy water!"

Father in his late seventies and rather gloomy, was nevertheless impressed: "Are Catholics always as cheerful as that?" he asked me. I said they were in Liverpool; but in Leicester they were apt to be more dismal.

But to return to Roche in wartime. In school the evacuees did not shine. I always felt that the girls were handicapped with Christian names like Lily and Nelly, which the Cornish had jettisoned fifty years before. When I went to grammar school also I was not in the least threatened by competition from London boys. A certain woman teacher with a cockney accent that could be cut with a knife used to say "Nauow you London boys, douon't let that Phillipps be top of the class all the toime".

But Granda Phillipps, at nearly eighty, saw things differently. "Are you keeping careful reckoning of your note-books, Kenneth?

I have heard that one of the London boys claims he is going to beat you by fair means or foul. So watch out."

It ill becomes me, who have fallen prey to paranoia occasionally in later life, to criticise my grandfather; but I can't help wondering where he got his information from. In any case I sailed through at this stage of my life with great bumptiousness; something I have since lost. Father would sometimes take me down a peg or two. When I boasted that I had a good memory, for example, he answered, "Yes, boy, so have Ralph Philp". Ralph Philp was a half-wit who could remember the first line of any hymn in the Methodist Hymn Book, provided you gave him the number.

I had sat for a scholarship to the St. Austell Grammar School in 1940, in the very depth of the Second World War, England's darkest hour. One of the few bright spots of that year was a raid in April 1940 in which a British flotilla forced its way into Narvik Fjord, in Norway, and sank four German destroyers. In the scholarship English exam we were told to write an imaginative account of this raid. I was rather proud of my bristly spelling to render foreign accents.

By September when I started at St. Austell, the war had been going for a year. The school, much bigger than any I had known, had its windows stuck over with strips of paper to prevent flying glass. Occasionally a former member of staff, called up, would wander reminiscently through the building in very smart officer's uniform; "Bettermost class of people", I thought. Patriotism was in the air: if we made a row between lessons we were told we were not 'good Britishers'. At the top of the playing fields with their splendid view of St Austell Bay was a long series of trenches, recently dug, and we went to them when there was an air-raid warning. At the end of one threatened raid lasting all morning, there was an unfamiliar sound of what seemed to be an alien aircraft, "Get right down in the trenches," said Mr Martin, our form teacher, "We don't know what this is!"

I suppose I was very lucky; it was the closest I came to combat!

Meanwhile in another 'sector', father had agreed, as the air-raid warden nearest the eighty-four foot high Roche parish church, to climb the tower in all air-raids, keeping a look-out for enemy parachutes. Half way up in his ascent the all-clear would tend to go. Few people were more ingenious than my father at finding ways of undertaking a task in a more leisurely way. He did not go right up the tower very often.

The first half of the war, till at least 1943, seemed to be a succession of gloomy disasters. This was brought home to me by the experiences of a Plymouth boy, evacuated to Roche and attending the grammar school. His father lost his life when the battleship *Prince of Wales* was sunk by the Japs in 1942. I admired the way he stood up to this. His name was Glanville, a very Plymouth name as a glance at the local directory will show. The most famous Plymouth Glanville was Joseph Glanville (1636-1680), a theologian whose *Vanity of Dogmatising* contains the story of 'the scholar gipsy', employed to good effect by Matthew Arnold:

> And near me on the grass lies Glanvil's book –
> Come, let me read the oft-read tale again!
> The story of the Oxford scholar poor . . .

There are advantages for non-combatants in wartime. One was the greatly reduced traffic on the roads. As a family the four of us used to go for cycle rides; preferably on the north side of the A30, which in mid-Cornwall even now is rural, not industrial. A rather silly headmaster I knew used to say that inland Cornwall was dull. More discerning was Sir John Betjeman, with his re-mark, 'Inland Cornwall is mercifully considered dull'. We used to ride through beautiful, but not sensational countryside (perhaps Matthew Arnold's word 'shy' would be appropriate); all not far from home: Withiel, Withielgoose, Grogley, Ruthernbridge. At Grogley, if the month were August or September, we would stop at the farm of Mrs Burgess (a customer), and she would spread a tarpaulin under a plum tree to catch the plums, which we would buy for making jam. It always seemed to be sunny weather as we went back to the little railway to pick up our bikes at Grogley Halt. It is 'all changed, changed utterly'. You could not leave cycles safely like that now; but in any case the railway, one of the prettiest, scenically, in the south-west, is gone.

Roche was too far above sea-level and too cold to grow apples; but the more favoured adjoining village of Withiel was in good apple country; and Withiel farmers sold quantities of fruit in our village. A Mr Sam Pedlar, with the careful vocabulary of the accomplished local preacher that he was, used to say: "I did not grow these apples; I can recommend them therefore, but I cannot guarantee them." A cousin of grandma's named Arthur Mutton[1]

---

[1] *Mutton* has always been a name of the Bodmin hinterland. It is intriguing that the inscription for the donor in one of the splendid early sixteenth-century windows of St. Neot's church bears this surname. The maiden name of my Knight great-grandmother was Mutton.

was another apple seller from the Withiel area. He came regularly but Doreen gave him many a baleful look. This was because the notable facial characteristic of all the Muttons was projecting teeth; and Doreen, whose teeth were at that time a little prominent, used to say, "I see how it will be; I'll end up with Mutton's teeth." There was also in the same family a noted local preacher who was particularly prone, as the vulgar say, to 'give her teeth an airing'.

Also on the far side of the A30 was Inches Downs, and the farm of Mr Roy Hawken of Kerriers. Again, at the time of the making of blackberry and apple jam, we would cycle there as a family and buy 'nawsies' as we called them; long-nosed cooking apples. We children were allowed to pick and eat as many of what Roy Hawken called 'grandfer's apples' as we liked. These were sweet but inelegant eating – I suspect they were rundown survivals of older varieties. It was understood that these little apples were to be eaten out of doors, partially chewed and then spat out, rather in the fashion of modern wine-tasting.

We must have seemed a happy family as we cycled home in these wartime days; pelting one another with the sticky burrs that grow so well on Inches Downs.

Sometimes my sister and I might be invited, through our Anglican cousins, to a dance at the church Sunday school. It was run by the Girls' Friendly Society, ruled by the irascible but likeable Mrs Tarplee, the rector's wife. It shows how hard up the GFS was for partners that I should have been invited; for I was hopeless at dancing. One simple dance 'Underneath the Spreading Chestnut Tree' I mastered; and that was all. Monica and Pamela were streets ahead of us; but then, ability to dance was an important part of Anglican doctrine.

But at least I behaved myself: 'Lennie, Lennie, Lennie!' Mrs Tarplee would call out, 'I will not have any of that roughness! Stop it!' That was Lennie Brenton, whose father kept the Post Office, and who is now a pillar of the established church in Roche, and, like myself, an old age pensioner.

Some years later, in 1944, just before D-day, the village was packed out with hordes of American soldiers. Dressed in uniforms of very good quality cloth, they made our soldiers look like peasantry. In those days, before the Victory Hall was built, the village school, with the partition screens pushed back, served as a dance-hall. The premises were, of course, far too small; especially with hundreds of G.I.'s crowding in. Towards the end of a Saturday evening it was like the Black Hole of Calcutta. Some Americans rightly demanded, and got, their money back.

Nor were the dancing partners, native girls, adequate; except that there was one strikingly beautiful Roche girl at this time. This was Uncle Wes's daughter, Pamela Kendall, now Mrs Pamela Julian. One G.I. was thoroughly smitten, but he spoilt his suit by neglecting his homework: 'You let me take Panama home tonight,' he told Pamela's mother, 'and I'll give you chicken and peaches in the morning.'

For once, Auntie Ella decided that discretion was the better part of matchmaking. She took 'Panama' home herself.

Father was shocked at this threat to his favourite niece; and equally disconcerted, perhaps, at the pernicious mixture of foods: 'chicken and peaches!' 'twas enough to give you indigestion just to think about it!

The Yanks, in their stay of only a few weeks in Roche, loved our shop; and since they had, as the saying goes, 'money burning holes in their pockets', they bought whatever they fancied and, I suspect, threw their purchases away soon after. There was only one complaint: one 'doughboy' rummaging among old stock found a padlock he liked and bought it; but shortly afterwards he returned, demanding his money back. On the padlock was engraved a swastika. Goodness knows how long it had been in the place, for some of our stock was really old, going back well before the Nazis rose to power in 1933. In any case Kipling's books often carried a swastika as what would now be called a logo.

Of course, the American got his money back. Father got on famously with them. They used to play extremely noisy games of baseball in the Recreation Ground, calling out "Let's go, let's go!" the same words, it is alleged, with which Eisenhower started D-day. One officer said to father, "Don't think too severely of the things they get up to Charlie. They all have it at the back of their minds that they could be dead in a few weeks."

Watching the recent commemoration of D-day on TV from Normandy I wondered how many of those delightful Americans were killed on Omaha beach, for example where there was a seventy per cent casualty rate on 'the longest day'. How many were lost elsewhere?

St. Austell Grammar was a cheerful school; when, on going to Liverpool University, I heard lurid tales from former pupils of some of the big Liverpool schools, St. Austell by comparison seemed exceptionally happy. Yet along with this went a capacity for selection and training. I was earmarked as an Arts student. A Mr Julian, better read than many physics masters of the time, having given me up as a dead loss to science, would draw two parallel diagonal lines across the board:

"That's an inclined plane, Phillipps: mean anything to you?"
'Not much, sir.'
"Does the road wind uphill all the way, Phillipps?"
"Christina Rossetti, sir."
"You've been swotting them up!"

At the end of May, 1944, just before D-day as it happened, some forty of us fourth-formers went from St. Austell to Penzance to help for a fortnight with the new potato harvest. It was a farm camp and we were put up in an outhouse at Trengwainton, seat of the Bolitho family. There was also a public school from Kent billeted in the servants' quarters. This illustrated the fine sense of social discrimination of a certain Captain Pollard who acted the part of an old retainer, like a hanger-on in a fourth- rate British film of the period. I still remember how annoyed I was when on my making some perfectly reasonable request he replied, "Well, my boy, there's one thing: what's no good can't come to no harm!"

'Picking potatoes', as we call it, was rather tedious work, and made more so when one of the regular farm labourers would throw a spud and call out "Pick up that tatie, boy." In Penzance they called them *taties*, whereas in mid-Cornwall they were *teddies*. I worked on the farm of a Mr Jelbert who was clearly wealthier than most of the farmers in the china clay area. He was also more forward-looking, with tractors instead of horses. There was a landgirl working on this farm, red-haired and from Roche, named Rhoda Varcoe; I think that she often worked in the farm kitchen and was in effect 'in service', though this was contrary to landgirl regulations.

On the first Sunday after D-day there was at the camp a general wish (it would probably not occur today) to attend Madron Church. As I walked there with Harry Woodhouse, my friend throughout secondary school and later, he wanted to bet me five pounds that the inscription round the clock that we could not decipher in the distance, did not say 'Guinness Time'. It didn't. The sermon was a blandly appropriate Anglican one on a text from Joshua.

This friendship with Harry Woodhouse, lasting well after fifty years, began at St. Austell and with music, because he played the clarinet and I, as a pianist, attempted, in Alice's words, 'all the rest'. For the first time, while accompanying Mozart's clarinet concerto, I realised the importance of interpretation as well as technique. Afterwards in the house on the Bodmin Road, St. Austell there would be tea, on a trolley not a table, with cucumber sandwiches; and these might have aroused my worst Phillipps instincts: 'It could disagree with you; you might suffer for it later'. However, greatly daring, I decided to 'tackle' (the word *tackle* is very Cornish in its heroism) cucumber sandwiches, and I have since 'conquered' my initial dislike of cucumbers. Harry's mother, a teacher in early life and remaining in her quiet way an educator, saw more than she 'let on': "Never eat what you don't want to eat, Kenneth," she said. But in any case, when I was at Bodmin Road or out with the Woodhouses on the North Cornish coast such things seemed trivial.

Sometimes Harry would come out to Roche. "Would you like to tidy this lot up, Harry?" father would say.

"When I've got a few years to spare," Harry would reply.

"He'll get on," father said afterwards, "he's got a sense of humour."

It was many years later, working on a book on the English of Jane Austen, that I came across in her depiction of Henry Tilney in *Northanger Abbey* the sentence that I have associated with Harry ever since: 'His manner might sometimes surprise, but his meaning must always be just'.

But to revert to the Penzance farm again – as we worked in the fields overlooking Mount's Bay we could see what Milton called 'the great vision of the guarded Mount'. It is clear from this and from some lines of Spenser that people were impressed by St. Michael's Mount even in times not remarkable for the appreciation of scenery. However, West Cornwall man has a sort of superiority complex about the beauty of Mount's Bay, among other things, that Cornishmen born further east can find irritating. The hundreds of Penwith and Kerrier are the toe and the heel of Cornwall respectively; and it can sometimes seem to the dweller in mid- or East Cornwall that it is here that the shoe pinches. The West Cornwall man can give the impression that a special ichor is distilled from there to the rest of the Duchy. Whatever this ichor may be it does not have a literary base: A.L. Rowse. Anne Treneer, Daphne du Maurier, Charles Causley, Claude Berry *et al.* are not writers from West Cornwall; and it is difficult to think of any considerable literary figure who is. It is true that it was in West Cornwall that Morton Nance, in the white heat of his imagination, invented a good part of the ancient Cornish language, but in the manner of things these days the Cornish language industry with all its rules and revisions seems to be organised from the less Celtic neighbourhood of Plymouth.

Professor Charles Thomas quotes a Camborne saying: 'Beyond Truro, where they d'have the treacle-mines' (i.e. nowhere). This, he said (in 1953) was the usage of older miners in Dolcoath Mine; but taken more generally, as I fear it often is, this self-assumed hegemony cannot be good for the county as a whole.

A few months after our labours in Penzance a group of senior St. Austell boys went in a lorry to Vault Beach, near Gorran Haven. The trip was under the supervision of Professor Charles Singer, historian of science wearing a cowboy hat, with his wife whose teeth projected enormously. We had to pick from the rocks a certain kind of red seaweed which, as I later discovered, was used in the preparation of penicillin, just becoming available and amazingly effective in healing war wounds, it was said. We had no trunks to change into and our clothes got very wet, but we soon dried. As we clambered back aboard the lorry Mrs Singer called out: "Bravo! I can see you must have a jolly good gym at your school." Bryn Lean said quietly to me, "I suppose there's some saps talk like that the whole time." Faced with the exuberance of some upper-class speakers of English, I know what he meant.

In the grammar school of course we learned French, which I liked though I made careless mistakes translating into the foreign language. Women took over many of the teaching posts during the war, and there was a very knowledgeable and cultured teacher of French who was the widow of an interpreter at the League of Nations in Geneva. Unfortunately, she could not control boys, who loved to 'wind her up' (as they say nowadays,) and to watch her face and neck change in colour from pink to scarlet, from puce to crimson, when she would call out "Boys, will you be quiet!"

I felt sorry for her, and annoyed that she should not be allowed to teach as well as she might. She wanted us to read Charles d'Orléan's poem 'Le temps a laissé son manteau', a celebration of spring. This, predictably, was a disaster. Teenage boys were as swine when pearls were strewn before them. But privately I translated the poem into not very good English verse, and she was delighted. However, there was a word, current slang in the school at St. Austell, meaning toadying, behaving obsequiously. The verb is 'to chough', spelt that way I think to connect with the Cornish red-legged chough, which figures prominently in the Gorsedd ceremony. I was, naturally, accused of 'choughing'; but I lived it down.

Father had a certain interest in boys' clubs, and during the war he ran one for a time, every Wednesday evening. Being a dutiful son, whatever moralists may say, can lead to all sorts of tedium. The activities of the club included six-a-side football, metalwork and boxing. I used to attend but always contrived to leave early. A Mr Thornton, from the Association of Boys' Clubs in London, came to visit very occasionally. There was a connection with Roche because his relative had been Augustus Vansittart Thornton who was still remembered as a lordly rector of Roche at the end of the last century. Roche was quite a rich living in the hands of the Clapham Sect. Church services in my youth were always comfortingly low owing to the influence of these evangelical patrons. Mr Tarplee always officiated in a surplice; but later the situation changed. "I see they do have up a collar and hames in church now," said father. A collar and hames is the big harness for a big carthouse; applied by father irreverently to High Church trimmings. Augustus Vansittart was probably not in the first rank of the Clapham Thorntons, as they are described by E.M.Forster in the life of his aunt Marianne Thornton. In any case Augustus was born too late for the heady days of William Wilberforce, Zachary Macaulay and Hannah More, all of whom Forster's aunt knew.

However tenuous the connection may be, I am pleased to note the link with that very congenial novelist, E.M.Forster. I have learnt more about writing English prose from him than anybody else, except A.L.Rowse.

Nevertheless, the Thornton who visited our club seemed to me rather a silly man. He let it be known about father that he liked 'the cut of his jib'. I suppose he thought that, since there is a lot of ocean around Cornwall such a metaphor would appeal. But, at twelve miles from either coast, Roche is not necessarily all at sea!

When I was in my early teens a small incident occurred which filled me with a pleasurable sense of identity. It was wartime and in St. Austell bus station buses were not clearly marked till the last minute before departure. But I knew the routine and was on the bus when I heard someone whisper: "Is this the Roche bus?" "I think it must be" said her friend, "because I'm sure that there gawky boy in the front seat must be a Phillipps."

I didn't mind being called gawky; this was more than offset by my being so decidedly identified as a Rocher.

Roche was fun for the most part, and St. Austell with the school was work; and I had a desire that never the twain should meet. But when I was about the age of thirteen something occurred to upset the balance and show me at my worst. Father had the knack of obtaining bicycles in wartime. Imagine my dismay as I walked up the lane leading to the shop one Saturday afternoon and came upon the headmaster and the French mistress trying out new bicycles! There was, of course, petrol rationing and so very few cars. They were pleasant people withal, but all my Roche liveliness had gone; I had fallen foul of what I call my 'ignorant Cornish peasant complex', though I never had it at school. Gormless answers followed gormless questions. With ideas of sanctuary in mind I found another customer to serve. When the visitors from St. Austell had gone I went home to tea and looked up my French dictionary: *embarrassment*: the French word was *gêne*. *Gêne* and I were old friends.

This kind of neurosis was lifelong with our family. Even my father, generally impudent, late in life confessed his feelings, or lack of feelings about this, to me. But he had a handy formula which he passed on to me: 'Those that matter don't mind; those that mind don't matter'.

Of all school subjects none improves with good teaching like mathematics. At St. Austell at the beginning of the war maths was taught by a master past retiring age, who had probably once been good. In an excess of patriotic zeal, and to avoid the necessity of thinking, he devoted himself mainly to growing vegetables in an extended school garden, digging for victory. He would sit motionless in a chair in class while we all worked separately; and if anyone asked for help he would call out, "Simple, boy, simple; common sense!" Then he would proceed to the business of the day, which was, "Any gardeners for tonight?" I suppose that if I had gone in for gardening my maths would have improved; but I had enough work of this kind at home to do and the whole exercise reminded me of Dotheboys Hall, in *Nicholas Nickleby*, with the schoolboys cleaning windows once they had spelt 'winder'.

He, like Squeers, was from Yorkshire and he departed when I was in the middle school, regaling us in his farewell speech with many facts about his county, such as that there are more acres in Yorkshire than there are letters in the Bible. And then a change for the better occurred with a master who came down, I think, from Sutton High School, Plymouth. He lived in Biscovey, in the environs of St. Austell; and of course we made every allowance for this. There was a rumour that he was 'a holy terror'. Yet suffice it to say that the warfare he waged was psychological (there was little or no threat of force). Yet he kept the potentially unruly forms he taught in total subjection.

I can still remember the peremptory, the minatory: "Step out in front all those that got the wrong answer". To the amusement of classmates one confessed one's errors.

"Whew!"

This was a familiar expression. It meant that he was world-weary of all the nincompoops it was his misfortune to teach.

"What's your name?"

"Phillipps, sir."

"I'll Phillipps you, my lad, in more ways than one."

This ploy had worked well with a boy called Prophet; not so with other names, though he kept it up. It was allowable to smile weakly, but not insolently, at Sir's jokes.

His language was rather bucolic at times, as when he gave instructions about geometry: "You can't do it without you blob in the dihameter. What have I just said, Phillipps?" "You can't do it unless you put in the diameter, sir." People had been shot down in flames for less. But all he said was, "Whew, I could have studied English, but I'm glad I didn't."

The psychological warfare continued: "I'll waltz you round the room in two or three minutes"; "I'll shake you up if you don't buck your ideas up". Only one quiet, strong-minded boy called all this bluff. When he (let's call him Tregaskis) was ordered to stand outside the headmaster's door Tregaskis rushed down in an unseemly scramble and made the deliberate mistake of going into the headmaster's room. He was hotly pursued by the maths master, calling out his name.

One of the things I later learnt from eleven years of school-teaching myself is that exceptionally good disciplinarians are not particularly popular with their coevals. They are apt to inflict their colleagues who teach after them with relieved but boisterous classes, on the rebound as it were. I think we may take it that the headmaster did not welcome the intrusion of either Tregaskis or the master.

Tregaskis was the hero of the hour; but I did overhear a conversation between two parents on Speech Day, which made me think: "He's the one for 'em; he'll stop their nonsense. Nobody don't get away with nothing when he's around."

And a few months later, looking at my undeservedly good maths result in the School Certificate (as it then was) I had to admit that they were right.

Next door to us in Trezaise Road there was at this time a couple named Strongman. His was a typical Cornishman's career. He had gone out to South Africa mining, as he said 'on the back of the

South African war'. Somewhere, perhaps in their native Zelah, he had married Mrs Strongman, who must have been beautiful and who still had a 'bang' on her forehead, as if she were an Edwardian beauty. Mrs Strongman died, and Mr Strongman scandalised the neighbourhood by visiting his mistress on the evening of the funeral. Mother looked after the widower well, expecting no reward; but she got one, or rather I did: a puppy-dog whose mother, Gyp, lived next door. Peter, as I called him, was a ratting strain, and from time to time Mr Strongman would grumble regretfully: "That dog would be good if only it had been well-trained". But I thought of Peter as (to use a horrible recent phrase) a 'fun' dog. When he came running to the corner of the house, turning the corner and coming back with joyous jumps to fetch me, I could never resist the temptation to go for a walk.

The Phillippses have often had dogs. Auntie Ethel had her poodle and Uncle David kept Alsatians; I once gave great offence by quoting from a manual of etiquette that all dogs are 'U' (upper class) except Alsatians. Auntie Edith too was very fond of dogs; she had an overmantel above her kitchen range made of what was then called American oilcloth and this she stuck all over with 'stramfers' (as we used to call 'transfers') of Alsatians, spaniels and other dogs. Over the years she had several dogs, the most memorable being Mickey, a curly-coated retriever sent down from Scotland. Consumer research and consumer protest were not well developed in the forties, but I reckon that that dog would qualify as a swindle at any time. To see it, and smell it, breaking wind and swinging its enormous curly-coated black backside around to the detriment of the crockery, was to be aware that Auntie Edith had (lit. and fig.) been sold a pup. The trouble was that Auntie Edith's motherly instinct was strong and she took to Mickey; after all, she had taken to me! Uncle Owen was less sympathetic: "Turn that bleddy dog to doors" he would say, in a fine dialect phrase.

Granda lived to be eighty; but at the end of his life he was not in good health. He had a troublesome skin disorder; 'water trouble', for which the doctor advised him not to be 'too modest'; and mouth ulcers. For these last he tried old-fashioned cooking, and particularly plain buns, or nubbies as they are sometimes called. I have seen granda look at a selection of these buns on a cakestand and carefully squeeze them all to pick out the stalest, which he would eat with a basin of cocoa, drunk by spoonfuls.

This dislike of 'the savoury' extended to his son, my father. But he, when he reached the age of seventy, boasted that he was more liberated in eating than most of his family: "Do you know,

Kenneth, I can eat a whole tomato now? Think nothing of it. Cut into quarters, of course."

Certainly, since both men lived to be eighty, there must be something to be said for plain buns. When my father visited us in the Midlands he always brought with him a supply of these buns, as, to use a dialect word, a stay-stomach; or perhaps they were an insurance, like a supply of quinine in the tropics. But the next generation is better trained. My wife says, "There is no reason to avoid eating something just because 'grandma's party' did not eat it!"

Even so, there are limits to my acceptance of 'the savoury'; H.P.Sauce, Daddy's Sauce, Branston Pickle and all such concoctions that are supposed to spice up but which really suppress flavour, these are things I cannot away with.

The same frugality obtained with drink. It was not enough to be teetotal: "I'm not sure," said father, "that drinking so much tea is a good thing." What he liked was a drop of milk, as for tea, and then to fill up with hot water. He was not alone. A Mrs Jabez Hawke, looking after her husband's welfare at a Faith Tea, would call out: "Milk and water for Jabez, please." This became a family saying that mother used in her more sarcastic moments: "Milk and water for Jabez!" I would have no truck with this. I used to argue: "John Wesley drank tea: even William Cowper would drink 'the cups that cheer but not inebriate'." I have read somewhere that three hundred years ago, when tea was an innovation, servants used to re-use the gentlefolks' tea-leaves to make more cups of tea. In my more cynical moments I am rather surprised that no-one in Cornwall continues this custom.

A rather Spartan diet might help towards a long life; but as far as granda was concerned there was another ingredient: willpower. Long after retirement age, during the war, he had a small meadow ploughed up and he 'put it to potatoes' as we say, for he was that rarity, a patriotic Phillipps.[1] Everything after ploughing he did by hand. If he harvested some really big potatoes they would be exhibited in the shop, perhaps on a pair of scales.

In 1946 I went to try for a scholarship at Emmanuel College, Cambridge. The subject that I have always considered 'my' subject was English. I would apply to the English master at St. Austell, Mr Holland (Duchy, we called him) if my marks for an essay were less good than usual. What a pain I must have been to a man who

---

[1] A local patriot, too. "I'm mighty glad Hitler didn't come," he said to me. "He'd have made some mess of our little Cornwall."

was very unwell and (though I obviously did not know this) was in fact dying. He lent me books, weaning me from the happy ending of the Sunday school reward by recommending Thomas Hardy; and he gave me excellent advice about style. When, in later life, pupils and students have demanded a lot, it was salutary to remind myself, 'Remember what Duchy did for you.' But by the time I arrived in the upper sixth he was dead, and I was given the Hobson's choice of applying for a history scholarship. My heart was not in this venture and I did not get an award.

When I came back to Higher Trerank granda was in bed with pneumonia; so ill that everyone knew he was going to die. Over his bed was a steel engraving of The Sermon on the Mount. He had been calling for me, Auntie Hannah said. In his hand he held a pair of silver watch-chains: "Two daicent chains – you must have them made up into one; we'm good for that sum; for I have always felt our future was bound up with each other, Kenneth." Somehow, though granda set himself the highest standards in conduct and craftsmanship, money seemed not to accrue to him. I did nothing about the chains; but I have always recognised in him the qualities for good or ill, that have made our family special; and I am happy to say so now.

For his last days, the doctor recommended that he should take whisky. Predictably, granda refused: "I have avoided it all my life," he said.

But for the old-fashioned Methodist there was always one departure from teetotal practice; one malady that could only be alleviated by homemade rural medicine. What if you were troubled by 'excessive looseness of the back passage', in the euphemistic phrase? What was needed was a screw-top glass jar, lump sugar and a gathering of 'sloans', that is sloes. Granda used to make his own 'sloany wine'.

Meanwhile, Doreen pursued her object of matrimony. It may be objected to matrimony as a career that there is no career structure. But this is to neglect the important part played by carnivals in Cornish villages. Like the Vestal Virgins in Rome, the carnival queen's role is threefold: first as acolyte, second as queen regnant, and third as a bringer-on of future monarchs. Many years after her reign I explained this to my sister, but she was not impressed: "You studenty sort of people don't know what you'm telling 'bout. I wouldn't care if Phillipp (her own six-year-old son) got a job in the claywork, rather than talk that kind of nonsense."

Cussedness often works in our family. Phillipp got a first in history and an Oxford D.Phil; a total justification, I should have thought, of matrimony as a career.

But not everybody succeeds in this way. Auntie Kathleen for example did not. "You want to watch it, Doreen," she used to say, "There's a pretty many of the Phillippses been old maids, you know," Doreen went to her first selection meeting for carnival queen rather casually. At the second meeting she was duly selected; but there was a snag; all the cloaks and dresses were worn out. More had to be bought, and father and mother came to stay with me in Liverpool, where I was a student, to buy them. They were greatly impressed by Lewis's: "That's some store," said father. Mother was flabbergasted at the expense of it all, but father did not mind the money if he had a chance to show off.

Back in Roche the dress was made up, and a still greater difficulty appeared. Those who know their Cornwall will not be surprised to learn that this problem was a moral one. The dress was of a Victorian design, but the neck was low and mother was uneasy: "'Twas all very well for so-and-so and so-and-so (naming two village women of no reputation) but 'twouldn't do for we." It was here that the new Rector's wife, Mrs Steward, intervened. She was a woman greatly admired: "There idn' no nonsense about she; she's a lady born". She taught art, part-time, in one of the St. Austell schools; and it was said she filled her bath with jellyfish and such to paint them as if in rock pools. With all the authority of a Rector's wife and a lady born, she placed the confident pencil-marks of the art teacher even lower than the original neckline. So that was that.

The coronation passed off peaceably. When Doreen made her speech (she had all her father's talent, which I have not inherited, for making speeches) somebody watching near me called out "Credit!" I knew I was in Cornwall, and all was well.

So granda died, and I took my Higher School Certificate (A-levels, they would be now) and went to Liverpool University to read English. The headmaster at St. Austell came from there. In view of his low opinion of inland Cornwall, I was not inclined to trust his account of the delights of Liverpool; and in this I was right. Liverpool I found, was a city of breathtaking ugliness, and Lambert Dive and I, who shared digs in Aigburth for a time, used to run 'hate seminars', as it were, abusing the place.

Altogether, I was not happy about further education, because I liked the work at the shop. One did not admit this in the county school, as one was travelling on the conveyor belt of ambition. But sometimes, a man from the backwoods would ask: 'Are 'ee goin' carry on your father's business, Kenneth? 'Tis very handy for the likes of we.'

It depends, I suppose, what you understand by 'the bettermost class of people'. Also the assumption is that if you are better educated, you have more choice of career; but being educated did deprive me of one option I would rather have liked. Father, of course, wanted me to go to university. He pointed out that I was not clever with my hands. 'Could you cut panes of glass, for example?' he asked.

So there it is. No less a person than the late C.S.Lewis, of 'Shadowlands' fame, has said that university lecturing was the only work he could do; and, in a lesser way, I dare say this is true for me as well.

Chapter 5

Chapel

Telle us some moral thyng that we may leere some witt.

The chapel the Phillipps family attended at Trezaise was quite
loftily situated. From the choir window there was an uninterrupted
view across the Cornish moors and farmlands ultimately to the
twin peaks of Brown Willy and Rowtor in the far distance. Looking
across this landscape one might well be put in mind of 'the Psalmist
of old': 'For the lines have fallen unto us in pleasant places; yea,
and we have a goodly heritage.' This was probably the most
frequent Old Testament quotation on Sunday morning in Trezaise
Chapel; and indeed most Cornishmen quietly congratulate themselves, and thank God that they live in Cornwall.

The special Methodist occasions of my youth made up a year,
if not a liturgical year, regular in its routines. To the Anglican
Advent at the beginning of December there corresponded the
missionary tea, perhaps with a missionary preacher and a distribution of missionary collecting boxes. With the limited vision of
dwellers in a small county, I fear that the Cornish on the whole
do not take to missionaries. My father used to say when he saw
the processions of yellow-robed buddhist monks in our cities that
this was their revenge on the missionaries.

Christmas was celebrated at home; except that parties would go
from the chapel to sing carols. Christmas carols, in Cornwall
suggest one name: Thomas Merritt, of Illogan. Recently I went
from Mount to nearby St. Neot to hear a cantata by him; but clearly
his strength was not in longer works, but in the briefer carols.

One has only to read the first chapters of *Under the Greenwood
Tree* to be aware of how uniform the process of carol singing has
been in the Westcountry over the last hundred years:

'Forty breaths, and then, "Oh what unbounded goodness" says
the chief carol-singer, William Dewey, in Hardy's novel of 1872.
"Come on in here, in the lewth" (shelter); "'tis lew as a box in

here." Mr Garnet Rowe in the same tradition (he is still with us at eighty-eight) would say in 1946. "Now, number fifteen, 'Lo the eastern sages rise' ". Then would follow one of those carols with both words and music in what might be called provincial Baroque, to an involved tune:

> Lo the eastern sages rise
> At a signal in the skies.

Some of us sang *signal*, others sang *single*. Charles Lee in his Journal noted this particular confusion in Cornish speech.

But the remarkable thing was that, being a Trezaise choir, and therefore Trethewey-trained, everybody, however much they were limited as to language, could both sight-read and carry their own part in the harmony.

Some of Merritt's work will go; but one carol I am sure must live. Mother used to sing it as she busied herself around the kitchen at Christmas time. It was 'Lo he comes an infant stranger – Of a lowly mother born'.

The most inappropriate ceremony was on Good Friday. Apart from the singing of Isaac Watts's hymn, 'When I survey the wondrous cross', the whole of the afternoon and evening of what was a holiday, after all, was devoted to our resolving 'never to touch the drunkard's drink'. *Drunkard* is one of those words, like *radiogram*, more or less out of date. When I said of somebody in Leicester, "Of course, she married a drunkard" I was told I sounded like a Victorian tract; I should have said 'a man with a drink problem'. I was fascinated to find, in Richard Hoggart's *The Uses of Literacy* the same teetotal choruses that we were brought up on:

> Dick and Jane you soon would know
> If you lived in Jackson's Row;
> With three daughters and a son,
> Dick he loved them every one.
> My drink is water bright,
> Water bright,
> Water bright,
> My drink is water bright
> From the crystal spring.

I wonder whether there are any flourishing Band of Hope groups left in Cornwall. Probably not; though when I spent a term of study-leave in Bangor (The University of Wales) in 1972 and attended a very enjoyable concert there one evening, I was told that the performers were so versatile because of the 'capelau y eisteddfodau y gobeithlu,' (chapels and singing contests and the Band of Hope), The Welsh for 'to hope; is 'gobeithio'. The Band of Hope had a similar function earlier this century in Cornwall. The theoretical purpose was the avoidance of 'strong drink', but a valuable and practical by-product was the development of talents in singing, recitations and what were called 'sketches', short plays often demonstrating the virtues of temperance or, better still, teetotalism.

Part of the process was preparing the young for signing the pledge; against drinking alcoholic liquor, smoking or (originally) taking snuff. The Secretary of the Band of Hope signed our pledges for us, because his handwriting was so much neater! When I told a colleague in Leicester this she quoted Wordsworth's *Prelude*: 'I made no vows but vows were then made for me'. Every spring the man from the Western Temperance League at Bristol came to give a talk illustrated with lantern slides. His name was Winkless. 'Winkless The Drinkless' Charlie Common called him.

But probably the biggest festival of the year occurred in late May, the Sunday School Anniversary. The fact that every chapel's anniversary tended to occur in late May would suggest that all Sunday schools were founded at the same time, which of course is nonsense. But late May or early June was a good time for the women to show off their finery; which was duly noted: 'I see she had up blew for Anniversary; another flam-new rigout; where the money do come from I don't know.' If trade had been good, or if I had grown a bit, I might have a new navy blue serge suit for Anniversary. If I did not get one, Auntie Ella who loved to tease, would 'wind me up': "People will say 'There's that Kenneth Phillipps with zackly the same suit he had on last year!' "

The chapel would be very full 'all packed in like herrings' for Anniversary. All pews would be occupied and, in that age innocent of fire regulations, extra seats were placed sideways down the aisles. When Uncle Will, in *Shiner's Poems*, pretends to describe an organ recital, what he is really writing about is an Anniversary congregation as seen from the choir seats where he himself used to sit;

> The chapel he was vull'd right up
> And saits put in the aisles,

When William Jan ded see the crowd
His faace was vull of smiles.

'Ee got up pon the organ stool
And started off to play,
His hand and shoulders rockin'
Like a boat out on the say.

He runn'd his fingers 'long the keys
And made some pirdy sound
And every mouth was gaaped abroad
To clunk the music down.

Clunk is Celtic Cornish meaning to swallow, a word wittily used here.

The word *choir* in Anglican parlance often seems to mean sideways seating; but for minutes before the service the singers in a raised chapel choir could pop up one by one, like pigeons in a fairground shooting alley. The sopranos as they made for their place in the front row might be conscious that eyes were on their hats. But they were in any case somewhat outclassed in song and in appearance by one of the Tretheweys, an outstanding soprano. She came only to the final rehearsal before the event, and seemed to know the choruses of Handel and Haydn by heart with no need of music. At the age of eleven I was most impressed, particularly when she appeared on the Sunday in a long lime-green satin dress. We had our sophistications in Trezaise!

Down in the classroom leading to the choir stalls above there would be a sense of tension. Soloists are not feeling very well: 'I haven't eat nothing for tea at all hardly'. A note with numbers of hymns is sent up to the organist from the special preacher. The organist, born a Trethewey of course, might be playing something even she had had to practise. But everyone had confidence in her; she had her letters.

I too was not very comfortable in the classroom before the evening service. As a seasoned soloist I should have to justify my position, perhaps by singing an obbligato. This word was much prized and given a dialectal pronunciation *obbligaiter*. In spite of the special name it tends to be in practice a rather florid descant. I was never very confident about vocal trampolining above the choir as they sing a well-known hymn tune. More pleasant to sing something less demanding but more musical; say from *Messiah* 'How beautiful are the feet,' with its pleasing musical switch from a soprano to a mezzo-soprano register. I sang this frequently; and I remember how furious I was when one of the more mature women altos would not let me stand up to the end of Handel's lengthy organ postlude, but pushed me down; "Well, I thought you'd been standing long 'nough, Kenneth." she said.

Feast week, eight days or so after anniversary and at the beginning of June, was, when I was a boy, a considerable event. The chapels and the parish church each had their special days of celebration in the week. Trezaise Chapel had a Sunday school procession, led by a prize silver band (all bands were 'prize silver' in public, though brass bands in private). There would be a lorry-load of small children and walking scholars bearing banners with the injunction to Peter: 'Feed my Lambs' and 'Feed my Sheep'. Somehow I never got the chance to hold one of the guy-ropes; and it now seems incomprehensible why I should have wanted to! Feast tea was rather splendid, as Sunday school teas went; and then there would be a distribution of the new season's oranges. Giving away feast, or feasten, oranges was a general custom.

In the village all through Feast Week there would be *standings* (market stalls). There is a Cornish proverb underlining the county virtue of stubbornness: 'Stick to your standing if you don't sell a ha'poth'. There would be established stallholders, like the Kinsmans, who made their own confectionery such as you never taste now; cinnamon rock, for example. As a small girl, my sister was thoroughly muddled: 'This rock is Kinsman flavoured'. At least one Kinsman became a Mayor of Bodmin; but they never served mid-Cornwall better than with their excellent confectionery. Another stallholder would be Mrs Udy, with what they used to call a 'withered arm', the staple price of whose merchandise was a 'aapmy' The Udy name is celebrated in an inscription of 1731 on a punchbowl and quoted in the EDD thus: John Udy of Luxillion his tin was so fine, it gliddered this punchbowl and made it to shine.

A further Feast diversion might be an escapologist, tying himself up in chains, performing near the chapel. The Trezaise trustees were never sure about this. The man wore only swimming trunks; but as his act was popular chapel funds stood to gain from a rake-off. The man stayed. In the evening sports were the thing for the scholars, while the band played lively music: it might include that favourite cornet duet 'Ida and Dot'. As the athletics dwindled the music changed to hymn tunes like 'Crimond' and 'Deep Harmony', while the rather chilly June breezes caused the standing spectators to turn up the collars of their jackets. One is supposed of course to prefer a symphony concert; but a brass band playing hymn tunes in full harmony conjures up my county like no other music.

The Thursday Feast of the parish church of St. Gomonda, Roche, used to end in the Flora Dance. I remember this particularly because in one of my adolescent years I was taking part in the Flora Dance when my braces broke. Nowadays, well beyond teenage embarrassment, I should say: "Excuse me, my trousers are coming down", and leave. But I was in a foursome (the Flora is danced by twos and by fours, alternately) with a woman of unexampled piety. I could not leave the set. I still do not know how I survived!

But at Trezaise Chapel, for the Wednesday Feast, the Flora was thought unsuitable; after all it was a dance. However, there was a curious ceremony or custom, now fallen into abeyance which I am proud to have taken part in several times. This we called the Snail Creep; but Miss Margaret Courtney, related to the Penzance banking family of Bolitho, thought she could improve on the name:

> In mid-Cornwall, in the second week of June, at Roche and one or two adjacent parishes, a curious dance is performed in their annual 'feasts'. It enjoys the rather undignified name of 'Snail's Creep', but would be more properly called 'The Serpent's Coil'.

Language is treacherous: her preferred term now suggests a particularly gruesome form of contraceptive!

Neither Miss Courtenay nor Charles Lee in his novel *Dorinda's Birthday* is very clear in describing this custom. Lee does better when he quotes in his Journal from Homer; first in Greek, then in Chapman's seventeenth-century translation (the book that so impressed Keats). The general principle of the Snail Creep was a spiralling towards the centre, and a spreading out from this tight centre, and Lee quotes Chapman:

> Sometimes all wound close in a ring, to which as fast they spin
> As any wheel a turner makes, being tried how it will run
> While he is set; and out again as full of speed they wound
> Not one left fast, or breaking hands. A multitude stood round
> Delighted with their nimble sport.

I think Lee is right to see a close parallel between the ancient

Greek custom of Homer's day and our Snail Creep. Homer's dance is obviously quicker; and he seems to have managed without 'standards' as we called them; men directing things with leafy branches of trees. I remember Mr Cliffden Yelland (who sadly died recently) doing so.

That the custom of the Snail Creep was ancient and authentic I do not doubt. In this matter of authenticity we have an expert guide in Thomas Hardy. Writing in his novel *The Return of the Native* he says:

A traditional pastime is to be distinguished from a mere revival in no more striking way than in this, that while in a revival all is excitement and fervour, the survival is carried on with a stolidity and absence of stir which sets one wondering why a thing that is done so perfunctorily should be kept up at all.

That was exactly the way we performed the Snail Creep in mid-Cornwall.

To continue with the chapel year, one Sunday in July was reserved for the annual distribution of Sunday school rewards. Curiously, I found that the presentation of a book was usually a disappointment for me. "Kenneth Phillipps", the superintendent would call out, "Sir Edmund Creasy, *Fifteen Decisive Battles of the World*." It sounded exciting! But as a nine-year-old, however hard I tried I could not penetrate that mid-Victorian verbiage.

But here father was at his best. He cared about reading. "Next time I go St. Austell I'll bring home a book that is not too old for you." Once I remember I got *Kidnapped* on the rebound. "You'm suffering, boy, because you'm supposed to come from a smart-ass[1] family".

His views on books and reading were his own. He was not an advocate of stoicism while reading: "I wouldn't give tuppence for anybody that wouldn't let themselves have a good cry over a good book." He disapproved of bookmarks: "If you're not interested enough to pick up where you left off, you should read another book."

In August the Sunday school and the choir departed on different

---

[1] I once spent some time translating 'always smart-ass', which seemed an appropriate motto for our family, into Latin; and arrived at '*semper meretricium fundamentum*. The words are equivalent but the syntax is not entirely satisfactory.

days for the sea. Inland Cornwall and maritime Cornwall have always tended to be separate entities, and the two met, if at all, on outings from inland to the coast. Lambert, my friend from Padstow used to say that on a Sunday school outing nobody wore what we should now call 'leisure clothes'; they wore dark suits as worn on Sundays, perhaps of navy blue serge, with black lace-up boots which they took off only to 'wash their feet' as the Cornish used to call paddling.

At midday there would be much taking-out of pasties, amounting possibly to a two-course meal; meat and potato for the first course, and apple and spice for dessert. A vacuum flask would contain tea: 'Nothing so well as a good cup tay'. A 'boughten' cup of tea might turn out to be 'water bewitcht and tay begritcht' (begrudged).

Members of the choir on their outings were more given to superciliousness than members of the Sunday school. They were mostly older and travelled further afield, perhaps to Ilfracombe or Torquay. When they were courting father and mother went on one such outing; and somehow they were offended. His opinion was confirmed that the choir was a 'click' (clique) and he never went again. These smouldering and at times rumbustious rows went on in all chapels; with the poor minister vainly trying to keep the peace. I sometimes think teetotalism sustained these long grudges.

Harvest festivals were nearly as important in the year as anniversaries. For these occasions the chapel would be richly decorated; and there would be ample opportunity for our noted Trezaise horticulturalist, Mr Tom Tippett, to display his begonias and other pot plants, which formed the centrepiece under the pulpit. Here too would be a large batch loaf, baked by Mr Tom Yelland. On various ledges and sills there would be fruit, prize vegetables and corn.

Tom Tippet's skill in gardening was obvious in Trezaise. His front room window was full of cyclamen, cinerarias and so on throughout the year. He did a brisk trade in pot plants etc. "That front room window is his shop window", father used to say. "He should pay extra rates. I got to pay for my shop window."

Sometimes in Cornwall these days, I feel I have lived for at least a century, so great are the changes. Tom Tippett was a local preacher, like his brother George, my great-uncle. Mrs Constance Rowe of Luxulyan confessed to me that as a girl she had been guilty of woeful ignorance. It was June and she sliced her father's new potatoes the wrong way. They were 'kidney' potatoes and should have been cut lengthwise, not across the middle.

But that was not the worst; for that day, as it happened, they had the preacher for dinner and the preacher was none other than 'Tommy' Tippett, as she called him (they were always rather less respectful in Luxulyan than we were at Trezaise).

What was to be done? Constance's father was in a quandary; there were some more potatoes not yet dug; but this was Sunday morning and the garden was near the public road!

I hope the reader is aware of all the moral implications here. Should Mr Stanley Roseveare break the Sabbath in order to maintain his standing with a leading horticulturalist? An agonising dilemma!

Constance has now lived down her error; and, happily for us all, is still living at the ancestral home of the Roseveares in Luxulyan.

But to return to the harvest festival, a special service on the Sunday afternoon might display the only art form that, as far as I know, Methodism has ever produced; this was the Service of Song. At harvest it consisted of a bucolic tale with a harvest theme, split up into episodes interspersed with rather mediocre tunes of devotional music. There would be plenty of chance for soloists. Something like this:

Caleb Dewhurst looked across his five-acre cornfield, nearly ripe unto harvest, and sighed. What a harvest! Never in all the years that he had been farming Little Puddlecombe had he known such a harvest . . .

This section would be read to the congregation; to be followed by 'Solo, with chorus': 'Cornstalks in God's field,' or something like that.

More satisfactory fare might come in the evening, with the singing of 'The Manx Fishermen's Evening Hymn' to the tune of 'Peel Castle' With this there was a separate verse for men to sing:

Our wives and children we commend to Thee
For them we plough the land and plough the deep;
For them by day the golden corn we reap
By night the silver harvest of the sea.

'Methodism was born in song' we are told; and certainly many Cornish Methodists would think that singing was the most important activity in going to chapel. It was only a few non-singers like the Phillipps family who rather disconsolately turned the pages of their humn-book during the singing. There are no longer many contrapuntal hymns with intertwining melodies, liked by the Cornish as long ago as the eighteenth century, though deplored by Wesley. But in Cornwall still, the tune for 'While shepherds watched' is nearly always Lyngham ('riding roughshod over the words' was Charles Lee's objection) with its repeated ending; and 'All hail the power of Jesus' name' is likely to be to the tune 'Diadem', even if it does involve a temporary separation of the sexes!

For my mother and father, growing up before the first world war, one hymn had a special emotional significance. It would be sung as the last hymn in chapel on a Sunday evening when a family was about to emigrate:

> God be with you till we meet again,
> By His counsels guide, uphold you,
> With his sheep securely hold you.
> God be with you till we meet again.

Certainly if the emigration were to Australia or New Zealand there would at that time be little hope of a reunion in this world. But the chorus of the hymn makes due allowance for this, and the characteristic intervention of the basses confirms it:

> Till we meet, till we meet,
> Till we meet at Jesu's feet
> (bass) Till we meet . . .
> Till we meet, till we meet,
> God be with you till we meet again.

Another hymn that I remember being sung with great apposite-ness was 'When wilt Thou save the people?' by Ebenezer Elliott, the Corn Law Rhymer:

> When wilt Thou save the people
> O God of mercy, when?
> The people, Lord, the people,
> Not crowns, not thrones, but men?

I remember the impression this hymn made in a packed Roche 'Wesleyan' chapel in 1938, at the time of the Munich crisis. Chapels could make a point in those days; but I am quite sure that Ebenezer Elliott does not appear in 'Hymns Ancient and Modern.'

Now that Methodists probably do not know their Bibles as well as they did a hundred and fifty years ago,[1] it may be that it is memories of the hymn-book that speak. About ten years ago in Leicester I was advising a Mrs Dorothy Grimes, who was embarking on a study of the dialect of her native Northamptonshire. A good deal of extra interest attaches to this dialect because the Victorian poet, John Clare, who lived in that county of spires and squires, used many local words. But Mrs Grimes was put off by the prospect of using the phonetic alphabet for her purposes. Would she confuse her work and muddle her readers?

There was something in her thought-processes that struck me as familiar. So I said, "I think, Mrs Grimes, you should regard phonetics in terms of 'earth's bliss' in the Methodist hymn-book: 'So that earth's bliss may be our guide and not our chain'.[2]

Mrs Grimes' eyes lit up. "How did you know I was a Methodist?" she said. "They sang that hymn at our wedding."

"At your wedding, Mrs Grimes?" I said.

"Yes", she said, "I was very strictly brought up."

And now she has raised a family; and in retirement has produced a splendid book, *Like Dew before the Sun*. She sent me a copy. I rang her up and said, "This is clearly a labour of love, Mrs Grimes."

"Yes," she said, "We Methodists can sometimes rise to a labour of love. And besides, it is possible to be in love with a dialect. Nobody should know that better than you."

There were some notable women evangelical hymn writers, some of whom seem to have been greatly influenced by the weather. Miss Frances Ridley Havergal for example, whose best known hymn is 'Take my life and let it be', would sometimes write a hymn when she was, as we were told from the pulpit, "prevented from attending divine worship owing to inclement weather". The American, Miss Fanny Crosbie, seemed to be of a tougher breed and lived to be ninety-five (1820–1915). It is said that she wrote eight thousand hymns, and for a time was under contract to a New York publisher to write three hymns or devotional songs a week!

---

[1] One reason for this is undoubtedly the woeful preference for what I call 'Cheerio' Bibles. To say, as I have often heard it said, that the Authorised Version of 1611 is incomprehensible seems to me a wilful downgrading of one's own intelligence.

[2] The penultimate Methodist Hymn Book, no, 379 'My God, I thank Thee who has made this earth so bright', by Adelaide Anne Procter.

So probably it would have been pressure of work rather than inclement weather that would keep her from her place of worship.

Fanny's 'Rescue the perishing, care for the dying' is perhaps now thought melancholy for general purposes; though it might be useful in checking the exuberance of a Sankey evening. As for 'Safe in the arms of Jesus, safe on His gentle breast' this is Victorian strong meat; too strong for our more delicate post-Freudian susceptibilities. I have never heard 'Safe in the arms of Jesus' on a television 'Songs of Praise'; not even when Thora Hird was in charge.

The aunt of my friend Charlie Common, mentioned elsewhere, knew her hymnbooks. I remember travelling home on the Roche bus from St. Austell when she was in the seat in front; but in any case it was easy to overhear her. As she knitted busily, she commented on her own efforts: "Miss Rose Hosken always says I remind her of a line from a Sunday school hymn, 'Give every flying minute something to keep in store' ".

How Arnold Bennett, who knew his Methodists, would have loved Charlie's aunt!

If a hymn had a chorus an encore was possible. An enthusiast like Mr Stanley Blight, with a revving-up of his vocal chords not unlike clearing the throat double forte, would start the chorus up again. It might be 'Showers of blessing' or 'From sinking sands He lifted me' or something similar.

We were often warned at Trezaise that once we started on any course we might not be able to stop. This was obviously true of sin but it was true also of repeated choruses. Once started they were not easily stopped; and only one voice was needed to scoop the tune up for a second time.

Or indeed, as in one instance, for a third! A young man of about twenty-five called Derek Yelland revved us up for a third time. There was nothing for it. Despite many giggles and some black looks we all had to follow. Derek enjoyed the situation enormously.

Not long after Derek was dead: he had an exceptionally thin skull and was killed by a cricket ball. No wonder I dislike cricket.

I was an exceptional Phillipps in being interested in music;[1] but most of the family were inclined, and perhaps expected, to display

[1] Old Mrs Rowse, who remembered the Crimean War, had no difficulty in accounting for this maladjustment: 'his great-grandmother Charlotte Trethewey, was a lovely singer; and used to sing solos up Trezaise in the eighteen sixties!'

their talents in one other special field. I once heard granda say, as he showed Newfoundland Phillippses around just before the war; "The Phillippses were not good at much but most of them could recite." I now see that this was the non-musical Phillipps way of keeping their end up in competition with the Tretheweys.

Two poetry books were prominent in granda's bookcase, both by American poets, Longfellow and Whittier, Whittier's most famous lines, becoming more relevant by the minute, are probably:

> Drop Thy still dews of quietness
> Till all our striving cease,
> Take from our souls the strain and stress
> And let our ordered lives confess
> The beauty of Thy peace.

But more recitable is 'Barbara Frietchie' with its 'now-read-on' or rather 'now-keep-listening' quality;

> 'Shoot, if you must, this old gray head,
> But spare your country's flag,' she said.

No poem was recited more frequently than Longfellow's 'A Psalm of Life':

> Life is real, life is earnest,
> And the grave is not its goal

and later:

> Lives of great men all remind us
> We can make our lives sublime
> And, departing, leave behind us
> Footprints on the sands of time.

In my autograph book father wrote this parody, which he had picked up somewhere:

> Wives and daughters all remind us
> We must make our little pile,
> And, departing, leave behind us
> Cash for them to live in style.

Grandma Phillipps believed, rightly, that more credit should be given to the memories of those who remembered passages of prose; but her favourite recitation was 'Billy's Rose' by George R.Sims, with its arresting beginning: 'Billy's dead and gone to glory'.

The recitation I found most exciting (it was an item at a concert I attended in the late thirties) was 'The Midnight Ride of Paul Revere' by Longfellow, based on an incident in The American War of Independence.

> He said to his friend, 'If the British march
> By land or sea from the town tonight,
> Hang a lantern aloft in the belfry-arch
> Of the North Church tower on a signal light,
> One if by land and two if by sea,
> And I on the opposite shore will be.

Beside 'Barbara Frietchie' for the American Civil War, there is 'Curfew must not ring tonight', a Victorian tribute to our own. This tells of how a young lady saved her lover's life, when he was due to be hanged by the Roundheads at curfew time. Resourcefully she made herself into a sort of human bell-muffle, so that the curfew could not be heard (it helped that the man who rang the bell was deaf). The direct if unworthy descendant is the pop-song, 'Hang on the bell, Nelly, hang on the bell.' Sunt lacrimae rerum.

These recitations are some of the parts of the canon of English literature that university teaching of the subject does not reach. I can illustrate this very precisely. A certain lecturer in history at Leicester approached her friend, Monica Jones (the longstanding companion of the poet Philip Larkin) with a quotation for her to identify. It was:

> I must go on with the service
> For such as care to attend.

Monica's friend had inquired in vain of a largish group of English lecturers assembled in the Senior Common Room; but Monica of course knew; and so, when she asked me, did I. "Read it?" I said, "I've recited it!" Owing to great-uncle Charlie, we had read Kipling's *Rewards and Fairies*.

Has this talent for recitation died out in general and with the Phillipps family in particular? It rejoices me to reply to the second question in the negative. To go, twenty years ago, to a concert in a certain Leicester girls' school was to find that Jenifer Phillipps was reciting one of her own poems. As with dialect poetry everything depended on the first impact; no self-indulgent meaninglessness, no faults of metre or rhyme.

As to preaching, this varied from extremely feeble to, at its best, inspired vernacular. Since such a number of Anglican clergy were non-native, the vernacular was rarely open to them as it was to the Methodist local preacher. One of the best I remember was the owner of a chipshop in the china clay area. He would come into the pulpit very formally dressed in a black coat and pin-striped trousers. Before preaching he would close the big Bible and hold up his arms in a nothing-up-my-sleeve gesture. The point of this of course was 'No sermon notes'. He would begin:

Brothers and sisters, you know me. I got a little chipshop over to Nanpean. One night I was on my way home from Plymouth with a load of potatoes for the chips. I overtook a couple going my way, that wanted a lift. "Where do 'ee want to go?" I asked them. "Don't knaw", they said. This was 'leven o'clock at night . . . 'Leven o'clock at night, and didn't knaw where they was goin'.

But my friends, isn't that like we today? Don't you feel 'tis 'leven o'clock at night? Do you knaw where you'm goin'?"

Preaching sometimes runs in families; and I have been solemnly warned by a young chapel-member at Mount whose wit is a continual feast. It started when I was asked to read the lesson at Christmas: 'In the beginning was the Word . . .' "You want to watch it", he said, "They'll have you up in that pulpit before you can say 'Jack-knife'. You say yourself that your great- grandfather was a preacher. The weakness is there! What'll happen is that the preacher will be took bad. Now they got sermons on tapes for this; but if they have to choose between a sermon on tape and a star of Radio Cornwall – I tell you, you won't stand a chance!"

But there it is; to use a dialect phrase, 'You can't odds it'. The later Phillippses have not the slightest desire to preach. Cousin Ruby said something that had the ring of truth; "Your grandfather was a good blacksmith, Kenneth I don't doubt; but really by instinct he was a scholar". A scholar in the days before scholarships and bursaries and grants.

But there is no question who I 'turn after'. Just as granda failed to make a big profit because he sharpened claywork picks and dubbers with too much craftsmanship, so I take great trouble over a book that perhaps nobody will buy. Neither he nor I have gone in for good works enthusiastically; but like him I have cared, in his words, for 'the little orphan knowledge'.

Being destined for a long wait in Lostwithiel recently, (and Lostwithiel, I think, still has the right to be called 'a quaint old Cornish town' as the song says), I went to the Royal Talbot Inn and fell into conversation about noted characters of the town; and particularly a Mr Beswetherick, who once kept a draper's shop there.

One of the drawbacks of living in a village in the old days, and perhaps especially during the Second World War, was the monotony of never seeing a fresh face. But to some extent, in chapel circles, this monotony could be relieved by a different local preacher each week. I am not claiming that Mr Beswetherick was as eloquent as the Charles Haddon Spurgeon (1834–1892) of the Metropolitan Tabernacle, about whom we were still hearing a great deal in the thirties. Still, he was a preacher who often came to Trezaise.

But, as dialect storytellers say, I'm a bit before my tale. As it happened, in my late teens I went to London with an under-graduate friend from Liverpool; and as it happened we went to Harrods. Harrods, that most opulent of stores, was enough to arouse the worst of my Cornish 'not-for-the-likes-of-we' syndrome. I remember thinking of *Alice Through the Looking-Glass*: 'The smoke in here is worth a thousand pounds a puff'.

Nevertheless, like many others who go to Harrods, I succumbed. Still on sale, to my great surprise, there were traditional Victorian snap-cards; the same pictures, the same captions. A Tudor courtier ('Your Majesty's humble servant'), a doctor in a nightshirt, called from his bed ('Who would be a doctor?'); most prominent, perhaps, a man who cuts himself while shaving his long chin, with the caption 'Another gash! oh my poor chin!'

Mr Beswetherick was planned at Trezaise one Sunday evening and I was walking home from chapel with mother. Like the Hawkens, and unlike the Phillippses, mother did not take much account of the 'ample page' of knowledge. But I do not see that there could have been a more Cornish family than the Hawkens and they had to the full the delightful vernacular trait of a sharp appreciation of characteristic detail in man and beast. It is precisely this that has given a great many comparisons, proper and improper, to the Cornish dialect.[1]

---

[1] In this connexion I always recall the remark about a man of surprisingly simian appearance: 'When thickey fellow start clapping for hisself, we shall know that he really is a monkey'.

Suddenly mother who knew the traditional snap cards stopped in the road and said, "Another gash! oh my poor chin!" She did not need to say more; we giggled all the way home.

For Mr Beswetherick, accustomed to 'plead with them earnestly, plead with them gently,' as the hymn says, would stick his rather prominent chin out over the pulpit in a not very successful attempt at a mini-Billy-Graham appeal. He would quote the hymn, 'Whosoever will may come,' and ask, "Will you be a whosoever?' I was troubled, not so much by the entreaty as by his grammar.

At the Royal Talbot I learnt from a Lostwithiel informant of how he went as a boy to buy a shirt from Mr Beswetherick. It was a question of choice. The shopkeeper said, "You take these three shirts home to mammy, my sonny, and leave her choose." As my informant said, nowadays that would be a sure way to lose three shirts. But in Lostwithiel in 1950 people were honest. Two rejected shirts went back to Mr Beswetherick. The boy was in a hurry because the 'do' where he was to wear the shirt was that same day.

But there was a snag. Mr Beswetherick had his own special cash-flow problem. Finding change from a note was difficult; money was kept in different piles in various places on the shelves, and these had to be located. My informant sighed: "In the end I was brave and late for that 'do'."

More than once I remember mother reaching for the preachers' plan on the mantelpiece: "Let's see who the preacher is next Sunday. Oh dear, Another-gash-oh-my-poor-chin!"

Where there is preaching, of course, there are always gaffes. My father delighted in a St. Dennis preacher who, he scandalously alleged, called out: 'Moses struck the rock, and water gushed forth! A miracle! After all, can anybody here make water?' I feel sure the man did not actually say this, but his general manner is shown in the way he embroidered on the text 'No man putting his hand to the plough and looking back is fit for the Kingdom of God':" "So I said to the ploughman, 'Ploughman, have you ever made a faux pas?" I must have been about fourteen when I enjoyed this.

One moveable event associated with preaching was looked forward to with mixed feelings in Methodist rural circles, and that was having the preacher for dinner. On the Saturday before, when the butcher's cart, (later van) came round, mother would say, "I want something a bit special; we'm having the preacher for dinner tomorrow."

The custom is not what it sounds like, latter-day cannibalism. Having the preacher for dinner meant a family's agreeing, on a rota, to take their turn in entertaining local preachers coming from a distant part of the circuit for Sunday lunch between morning service and 'addressing the Sunday school' in the afternoon; and also for tea, between Sunday school and evening service: "May we all come back 'gain in the evening and have a good time", was how one local preacher always ended the benediction at the close of the morning service.

I cannot say that I looked forward to our having the preacher; somebody had to say grace, for one thing: "Kenneth, will you ask a blessing?" Then father had an infuriating way of displaying my talents in reverse, by saying to the preacher, "Of course, he's a bit backward at school". The preacher would say comfortingly that many people who were low in class turned out to be noble souls. Then father would say after all that I was well up in class. I hated this silly ploy which he tried more than once, and I ought to have nipped it in the bud. But there was often an amusing side to having the preacher; one Sunday the as yet unmarried Uncle David came up from Higher Trerank to our house, exploding with laughter. At tea-time the preacher had helped himself (presumably by accident) to a huge section of round cake – all, in fact, that was unsliced!

Transport for the preacher was motorised by the thirties; but talking to a distant (Pentonvale) Phillipps relative, I learnt that earlier than this Pentonvale hired out their pony and trap for the preacher's travelling. The account was made out to the Quarterly Meeting; hire of the pony etc. was four shillings a quarter.

Margaret, Lady Thatcher, a former Methodist, has said that Methodists attend chapel too much. For once, I am in agreement with her. In our early teens my sister and I attended three times a Sunday, and whiled away the time between afternoon Sunday school and evening service by changing the water in the goldfish bowl. When I told a certain cynical friend he asked, "Was this a Methodist ceremony, too?"

In fact this 'ceremony' was the occasion of some rare mischief on my part. My sister Doreen was pouring the water and I tipped up the jug from the bottom, all over the floor. Father called out, "Kenneth; over stairs!" and I was sentenced to solitary confinement, but this was commuted to a couple of clouts across the ear.

Curiously enough, when we were a good deal younger the atmosphere was rather more relaxed. In chapel time father would play the gramophone; records like 'When father papered the parlour', but eventually mother would call down from upstairs where she was making the beds, "Charlie, they'm coming down from chapel. Play hymns!"

At Sunday school the advice was wide-ranging and varied; like 'It will save you from ten thousand snares to mind religion young', and 'if you got a watch, let your daddy wind 'un up for 'ee, or else you'll break the spring'. Father taught the senior boys one week in three. Considering that he had always had ambitions to be a teacher, I did not think he taught very well. Garrulous people rarely make good teachers; it is lawyers who are credited with effective talking. 'He do talk like a lawyer' is a common vernacular compliment.

Still, father was better than the redoubtable Aunt Huldah, who taught further down the school. The original Huldah, 'Huldah of old', as we perhaps should call her, was a prophetess mentioned in 2 Kings 22. It fell to her lot to have to cope with Hilkiah the priest, and Ahikam, and Achbor and Shaphan and Asahiah.

They cannot have been the easiest of people to get along with! I can well imagine, indeed, that it is their lineal descendants who pop up on our television screens from time to time when incidents occur on the Gaza Strip, or elsewhere. But my reading of this chapter in the Bible tells me that Huldah of old managed to straighten a few jackets, or Old Testament jacket equivalents.

I feel sure that in her prime our Trezaise Huldah would not have discredited her namesake in such matters; I have heard on the best authority that as a secular pupil teacher in Roche primary school (she went back to that era) she ruled her classes with a rod of iron. When she taught me in Trezaise Sunday school she must have been, as we say, 'beating on for eighty'. Huldah is Hebrew for 'weasel', but what with her small Trethewey frame, round shoulders and rapid movements on tiny feet, she looked (as I now see, not having then read Beatrix Potter) like Mrs Tiggywinkle in mourning. She read to us from American salvationist tracts of about 1880, I suppose. There was a certain unwelcome inevitability about these tracts. It happened too often, it cannot have been a coincidence, that to be 'saved' at one of the numerous mission-halls of, for example, Chicago, meant according to Aunt Huldah's book, that you took your life in your hands in the streets of the city afterwards. You might soon be the victim of an accident (if that was the word for it) as a result of the lethal Chicago cars. Cars were not, she explained, like our cars; streetcars they were sometimes called in Chicago. As Aunt Huldah read on about the poor young people who were first washed in the blood of the Lamb and then mown down by Chicago juggernauts, I grew uneasy. What made me feel especially uncomfortable was that Aunt Huldah didn't seem to think it was important, as long as you could 'see your title clear to mansions in the skies', whether you departed this life early or late.

I said to Charlie Common, also in Aunt Huldah's class: "We'd better give Chicago a wide berth".

"It would be OK", said Charlie," as long as you weren't saved!"

Aunt Huldah ventured into commerce in a small way. She ran a little shop in Trezaise. No doubt one of the staple items would be yeast. It is hardly possible to exaggerate the importance of yeast fifty years ago. There would be a large pie-dish full of yeast on every grocer's counter, however tiny the shop. Give a seasoned shop-assistant like my mother a sizeable sheet of greasproof paper and with a flick of the wrist she would turn it instantly into a triangular-shaped yeast packet. The process of making home-made bread and cakes is less common but not, of course, dead. When I rang Mrs Vine, of St. Austell, recently about genealogical matters, I asked if I was intruding: "No," she said "but in ten minutes I should have been wetting up some white yeast cake". From then on I proceeded with confidence.

There was another important item in Aunt Huldah's stock. This would be plans: 'The new plans are come and can be had from Mrs Trethewey, price twopence". I now pay 20p for a plan; but that, I suppose, is inflation. *The English Dialect Dictionary* defined *plan* as 'The annual arrangement for providing Methodist or Bible Christian preachers in the several circuits.' The EDD appeared in 1905; two years before the amalgamation of West-country Methodists occurred. The EDD might have added 'the document which publishes the arrangement'. For that, of course, is what Aunt Huldah sold. The plans really had, in the old days, a plan-like appearance, opening out again and again like a map and divided vertically by Sunday date and horizontally by chapel. All Methodists are familiar with plans, but the more elaborate plans are essentially rural documents; blueprints for chapel arrangements in a wide circuit that contained too many 'wayside bethels' to be visited frequently by a paid clergyman.

It was said of a certain courting couple in Roche that they would sit hand in hand by the hour, reading the plan!

Aunt Huldah had a rival in the piety stakes. This was the aforementioned Mrs Jabez Hawke. She was probably the last woman in Trezaise to dress as grannies traditionally should: like Old Mother Riley of music-hall fame. There is a masterly discussion of grannies in Laurie Lee's *Cider with Rosie*. Mrs Jabez Hawke dressed always in black, shining and glossy (whereas Aunt

Huldah had more of a matt finish as decorators say) with long skirts and long elastic-sided boots. She did not however wear a bonnet, as Lee suggests is proper for grannies, (and indeed as the popular name for the plant aquilegia, grannies' bonnets, implies). Mrs Hawke wore a hat, of bigger circumference at the crown than at the brim, which made the hat like the top-heavy headgear of the grandees of the Russian Orthodox Church.

She ordered a special door-latch and I had to deliver it to her house, under the very eaves of Trezaise chapel. Her turn of phrase was redemptionist: "What is the cost?" she asked. As an answer I felt that 'one and eleven' was altogether too mundane; and anyway I had no change. So I said, "Perhaps you had better see father, Mrs Hawke".

Everyone has at least one 'day' in their lives; and I suppose Mrs Hawke's came late: in the late thirties in fact, when the trustees of Trezaise Chapel threw away their oil lamps and installed electricity. As soon as I wrote the words 'threw away' I realised I had made a mistake; the oil lamps would, of course, have been sold to a smaller chapel.

But the day of the inauguration of electricity was auspicious. The afternoon began with a tea; not by faith but by ticket, and of two kinds, ordinary tea or high tea. I remember this arrangement only on this occasion. High tea was meat, salad and teetotal trifle, I believe. I say 'I believe' because the Phillippses would obviously not eat such things: "bad enough to have an upset stomach without paying extra for it."

When we all walked from the Sunday school to the chapel only the side lights were switched on. Mrs Jabez Hawke stepped forward and into the pulpit. In a surprisingly loud voice, and with that sense of drama that is every true Methodist's heritage, she called out: "And God said, 'Let there be light' and there *was* light!" At the word *was* she threw the big switch and the packed congregation, newly illuminated, burst into fervent applause.

These improvements must have put a great strain on the resources of the chapel, but this is a field where Methodism has long been known to excel. In my childhood fifty years ago one of the things to be seen at all feasts and celebrations was a man going around with a box collecting for the 'cause'. That always 'belonged to it', as we say.

The word 'cause', by the way, was a potent one. 'How's your little cause down Nanstallon?' – such was the frequent question. The chapel and all that pertains to it is the 'cause'. I was staying with Auntie Edith, at the age of nine, when I heard on the wireless a 'trailer' for the broadcast of Shakespeare's *Othello*. Othello calls out 'It is the cause, it is the cause, my soul'.

I decided that Othello must have been a Methodist; converted by our missionaries, probably.

Sharing meals is a long-standing Methodist tradition; and by far the commonest event of this kind until recently was the Faith Tea, usually held in a Sunday school. Very occasionally, in fine weather, I have known Faith Teas to be held out of doors; notably for me in a certain Bodmin Moor village forty-five years ago, when, tired and hungry from cycling and with no hope, as I thought, of refreshment, I came upon the answer to my prayer: 'refreshments by faith', as the formula went. The village was Mount, and forty-five years later I live there.

The food would be paid for twice: by the initial provider and by the eventual consumer. Proceeds for chapel funds. It tended to be 'cakey-trade' (cakestuffs) – and not sweet cake but yeast cake, both white and saffron. Quiller-Couch, in one of his short stories, describes a Faith Tea in the china clay area as 'fattening'. But clearly the Weight Watchers have now done their work. Recently, on Good Friday 1993, I attended a Faith Tea in Gunwen (Luxulyan) where there were meat sandwiches and generally a better balanced diet.[1]

Trezaise being a very musical chapel, the proceedings began with a sung grace: 'Be present at our table, Lord' to the tune of Rimington. All the four singing parts would come spontaneously. Tea would be served on trestle tables by 'tenders', a dialect word meaning those who 'tend table'. A separate table would be reserved for 'cutters-up', the wholesale department, so to speak, cutting up cake and spreading butter and jam 'splits' (round bread rolls). Laden plates would be handed to the 'tenders' who also had the important responsibility of pouring endless cups of tea. When I was in my early teens I remember watching, hungry and mystified, while a young newly-wed cousin of mine spent what seemed like hours proudly arranging the silver teaset she had brought, straightening the traycloth and so on, before the tea could begin.

There might be as many as three sittings at a Faith Tea, and father, who looked at these things with the jaundiced eye of the

[1] The most expensive item of diet in my childhood was 'butcher's meat', a phrase fairly common in Victorian novelists like Trollope. This accounts for a certain protein deficiency in some Cornish constitutions. The phrase 'butcher's meat' was partly in contrast to home-cured ham, etc., from the last pig-killing.

dyspeptic, said that one old man ate his way through all three. "Mind, I never think", father would say, "that what you eat outside is so well as what you do eat home." In contrast to the greedy man just mentioned, Miss Richards in the infant school ordained that we should eat a good tea before we went to a Faith Tea, and only eat one piece of bread and butter when there; thus helping chapel funds. I was an earnest disciple of Miss Richards; but I am pleased to say that I disobeyed this decree.

There were proprieties attending a Faith Tea; "If you'm in business somebody got to go to the tea to represent us". I have occasionally taken on the role of a plenipotentiary in this matter.

When I was younger and had little money (though a Phillipps is never as poor as he thinks he is) I looked long and with great interest at a display of Nonconformist china in a Newquay antique shop window. Unless our name is Micawber, we generally regret our economies more than our extravagancies. I do in this case. Commemorative chapel china in the china-clay area especially attested the connection betwen mid-Cornwall and the potteries of Stoke-on-Trent. Centenaries of chapel foundations were marked with mugs; John Wesley figured in Staffordshire ornaments, though perhaps we should not describe a 'cloam' bust of Wesley by the dialect word 'a joney'. The cups and crockery at chapel teas were usually fine bone china, doubtless bought from Staffordshire at favourable rates.

Sunday observance in the thirties, was not so strict as it had formerly been, so everybody said. Formerly some chapel members would cut a cabbage on Saturday night and leave it on the garden path to avoid unnecessary work on the Sabbath. Yet still when I was a boy, Mr Jim Burdon used to chain up the swings in the 'recreation ground' on Saturday nights and unlock them on Monday mornings. Certainly, when we had the preacher for dinner, our sabbatarian inactivity was exemplary!

If a Sunday school superintendent addressed the scholars and told the tale of a boy who had 'minchied', (our Shakespearean dialect word for playing truant) from chapel to go to the beach, you knew it was all up with him. Sure enough, a stone would fall from the cliff or a cave roof and he would be brought home injured but repentant, expecting to die an uplifting death.

Charlie's aforementioned aunt was a noted and incisive local preacher. Charlie was not very happy about her, I think because her sanctity had been too rapidly acquired and was too uncompromising. In one sermon I remember she told of a man whose friends deserted the chapel on a Sunday to go for a walk. "Lock up your valuables" the man warned them, "because if you break the fourth commandment you cannot blame anybody for breaking the eighth." I thought hard about this. The assumption seemed to be, according to Charlie's aunt, that all the commandments were of equal importance. This I decided was not so. If you were tempted to kill somebody, it seemed to me there would be a lot less fuss if you changed your mind and decided to covet his ox instead.

We were never, of course, rich; but when in the fifties and sixties we became a bit more prosperous, mother characteristically found a way to give some of this money away. She took to stripping trees.

This sounds like the worst excesses perpetrated on Brazilian rain forests; but I am writing of the fifties, not the eighties and nineties. Stripping a tree was a fund-raising device for a chapel. A small fir tree was decked with envelopes containing money given by chapel members and well-wishers, and these envelopes would be tied to the branches. The stripper (absit omen) would open the envelopes one by one on a public occasion, calling out the amount in each, to greater or less applause according to the size of the contribution.

Mother officiated at quite a few tree-stripping 'efforts', as they tended to be called. The tree-stripper was expected to have a 'long purse'; and mother no doubt would have given generously. Father used to say she was like Mrs Jellyby in Dickens' *Bleak House*, neglecting the family for good works abroad; but I think he was proud of her ventures in this field. Naturally she came in for some teasing: "You'll be had up by the Forestry Commission for destroying their property!". But mother, like her mother-in-law, did not mind being teased.

It was being Methodist and also teetotal that lifted us from working class to upper working class; a level of society that has always seemed to me the most desirable, though I have since been promoted out of it. There are fewer overheads than in the middle classes and fewer inhibitions. In our small circles we were people of light and leading. Middle class chapels did not suit father: "Too many fur coats in that chapel", he said of Leicester's refined Bishop Street. (He certainly did not disapprove of the coats on ecological grounds; he was furious when gin-traps were made illegal.) So when mother and father came to visit we attended Humberstone Road and 'sat under' as they used to say, a very good preacher indeed in a left-wing tradition, Rev. Mr Tongue. His appearance nevertheless suggested to mother undernourishment: "He could do good with a square meal", she thought. He filled in his time, to use a dialect phrase, by studying for a post-graduate degree in sociology at the University; and I wouldn't mind betting that there would be those in his congregation who would think this the equivalent of eating the bread of idleness.

No-one these days, I suppose, grudges the minister his or her meagre salary. Formerly things were different: as a curmudgeonly chapel brother is alleged to have put it, none too happily: "You ministers is paid to be good; we'm good for nothing." Father used to say "Wheresoever two or three chapel people are gathered together there you'll find the ministers being run down." Only rarely did a Methodist minister stay long in one place in the old days; but even at that time the brothers Joseph and Silas Hocking, who had both been ministers in Cornwall and elsewhere before becoming popular novelists, delineated the minister's career: first year idolised, second year criticised, third year scandalised. That things have changed is due partly to indifference, especially among the increasing non-native element in the population. There must, I suppose, be incomprehension too. Few know of, or are influenced by, that frequent judgement of the past, 'He's a wisht hand at the visiting'. Few now can even assess whether, in the vernacular terminology, a minister or any preacher is 'handsome', 'bravish' or 'wisht'.

Yet the surprising thing is that I am quite sure that Cornwall has never been better served than by the Methodist ministers of today. For one thing there is no pomposity now. I remember a highly regarded superintendent minister referring in a sermon to the enormous engine-rooms on the liner Queen Elizabeth (it must have been about 1940) and declaiming, "The spirit of God is in the wheels – in the wheels!" Already my mordant Phillipps mind had decided that the man was a windbag. Modern-day ministers are obviously not in the job for the money or the status. How those who are fathers of families manage I do not know; but there is also a very dedicated and competent type of woman minister. Any Methodist of Bible Christian extraction at least who objected to the latter would have no sense of history. The Bible Christians were noted from the beginning for their female preachers.

Not least of the recommendations of the modern Methodist minister is that he or she is alive to the needs of the young. How father, who was always associated with Methodist and other youth clubs, would have approved! He used to say that old people who merely prayed with other old people were really eating the seedcorn: "What sort of chapel will you have in thirty years' time?" he would ask.

The old people at Trezaise Chapel, thoroughly inert, did little during the war to further relations with those in the forces stationed elsewhere. It was left to the Wesley Guild, a young people's club, to do this. They ran large sales of home-made Christmas toys to provide parcels for loved ones. Here was no ordinary charity: but everything that was dear to a Cornish heart, 'looking after your own', 'within the family', so to speak. Letters were received in return for the parcels, and read out in chapel. A magazine called 'The Guild Gazette' was typed and duplicated and sent regularly to those in the forces and in munitions up the country. It was something to keep father busy when he wanted something more intelligent to do than checking invoices.

In the Gazette there were bogus adverts: for the profane Brice Yeo as a teacher of languages, and for the extensive Phillipps' showrooms along the side of the road. And here was Uncle Will, advocating a non-aggression pact with 'Lainer', a Hensbarrow man named Lean whom he saw as a potential ally of the Axis. 'Lainer' travelled everywhere on a motor-bike, with his cap, as we say, 'foreside back' i.e. back to front (it is a fashion that has come in again in recent years). Did we realise, said Uncle Will, as Trezaise people, what we were doing? We were robbing Hensbarrow of thousands of hurts (whortleberries) every year. Surely the answer was to ward off any retaliatory hostility from Hensbarrow by approaching Lainer with a non-aggression treaty. In return for the hurts there could be a trade agreement, with glass from the glass-mine (an old felspar quarry) and the odd product from the Polpuff scavenger (rubbish) dump.

At the end of the war the Trezaise Guild ran a big birthday party for all, with separate tables for those born in different months; and this event achieved the accolade: we had our photos in the *Recorder*: – that is *The Methodist Recorder*. This, we thought, was not bad for a hamlet the size of Trezaise. No comparable event occurred in Roche; but then, Mr Lean, the schoolmaster, had flattered us by saying that most of the intelligent children had come from the Trezaise end of the parish.

Intelligence in Trezaise would include that woefully neglected subject, Biblical knowledge. When, many years later, I read in an undergraduate's essay that Christ was crucified at Calgary, I reflected that he ought to have gone through Trezaise Sunday school. At that Sunday school nobody burnt joss-sticks or played a guitar to us; still less did they proclaim that Enoch Powell was Antichrist; but I still know how it is that Methusaleh, the oldest man who ever lived, yet contrived to die before his father; and how it came about that out of the strong came forth sweetness.

Chapels tended to be run by prominent families. Thus in the Bodmin area there were always Tretheweys at Trezaise, Richardses at Stenalees, Blakes at Retire, Jorys at Mount, Littletons and Roseveares at Bridges (Luxulyan) and so on. Many of these chapels will have been small, originally Bible Christian foundations; and now, too often, they have closed or are closing their doors. The statement 'Small is beautiful' applies to nothing more appropriately than to the Cornish Methodist chapels. When I think of Greensplat, Enniscaven, Mount and perhaps above all Gunwen, I feel resentful that there should be *yet another* guide to Anglican churches in the county, and that these lovely little buildings 'unwept, unhonoured and unsung', are bound to close. There ought at least to be a book of photographs with a commentary.

The 1935 Kelly's Directory of Cornwall lists six Methodist chapels for Roche. Now there are only two, Roche and Trezaise; the other four, Tregoss, Belowda, Mount Pleasant and Tremodret, are gone. The last is now a dwelling-house, though the owner had to fight a legal battle with a clay company to effect the conversion. Tremodret was very much great-uncle George's chapel, and I was sometimes asked to sing there. There is a fine painting of 'The Bible Christian Chapel, Tremodret' done by Ruskin Spear when he lived in Roche during the war. It is reproduced in a Pilgrim Trust volume *Recording Britain* (1949, vol. 4). That was fifty years ago; but we still have not caught up with the insights of this fine painting and continue to turn chapels into chipshops.

Mount Pleasant Chapel was very remote; in the neighbourhood of what was originally called the Bodmin Beam Transmission Station, but is now called 'Wireless'; a rather drab moorland situation. The place never had the benefit of electricity; instead, 'the Mount Pleasant Congregation', as we called her, used to come to the shop bearing an empty paraffin can. I suspect that she must often have worshipped alone. Father would always give 'the Congregation' her lamp-oil without charge.

Sadly, Bodmin circuit has been dismembered as a result of recent contractions and economies but its imposing chapel, Bodmin Centenary, remains. A preacher once wrote thanking my mother and father for hospitality, and proudly ended the note: 'Wor at Centenary last Sunday'. One wonders how they all got on!

Everybody is agreed that funerals play a prominent part in Cornish life. Motives for attendance are mixed: there was a lively but tactless Trezaise woman who said: " 'Tis good to go to a funeral to see some of your friends". Others allowed that there was a certain necessity about funerals, reasonably enough, because they followed death. An elderly Trezaise Methodist, having watched many Westerns, felt deprived: "Lots of people get shot but you don't see many funerals." (I dread to think what any Western she directed would have been like; one hears of 'spaghetti' Westerns; and I can imagine a grotesque 'pasty' Western with endless funeral processions, and six-shooters blazing over the coffins.)

One of the worst examples of misunderstanding of 'we Cornish' occurs in Father Walke's *Twenty Years at St. Hilary*: he overhears snatches of conversation among mourners after a funeral service. 'Have 'ee tealed your taters' or 'bullocks are fetching a poor price'. This proves, says Walke, that they are back again in the life they know. It is his opinion that 'their religion offers little to sustain their flickering faith'. The point is surely that these people in their grief are attempting to regain a sense of reality, which includes crops and cattle.

Kinship was seen as all-important, particularly at village funerals in a walking procession, though the tradition has dwindled through the hiring of cars and the prevalence of cremation. To go to a Cornish funeral of this kind in the old days was to see Celtic principles of kinship asserted: first of all instinctively at the beginning – and if necessary afterwards by way of reproach. Then one might hear a fairly common phrase: 'he or she was too far 'fore' (forward). It meant that husbands and wives did not necessarily walk together. The offence would be that someone of more distant kinship had followed too close to the coffin, and this might cause the displacement of some closer relative; though in fact the priority is largely intuitive where everybody knows everyone else. Of course the process is one hundred per cent Celtic.

One Sunday morning early this year (1994) I joined 'the society' at Mount Chapel as usual. The preacher was a Mr Peter Halls. Mount was originally a Bible Christian chapel, and Mr Halls preached a Bible Christian, nay a Bryanite, sermon. As we left at the end of the service I saw a boy of about twelve carrying a wooden box carefully. Thinking genealogically, as one can do in a small village chapel, I worked out that his surname was Best.

My friend Mr Little, a very lively eighty-year-old said to me: "He got two ferrets in that box. He's goin' to turn 'em goin' ".

Master Best did not in fact 'turn 'em goin''; but he opened the lid and everybody, as they came out of chapel into the winter sunlight, admired the little animals.

Mr Halls, a farmer from the Bolventor area, proved that as well as handling a text in a sermon, he could handle ferrets in a box: "You must put your hands firmly on their heads," he said. "If you approach 'em too cautious, they'll bite 'ee."

In my more cheerful moments, as when looking at these ferrets outside Mount Chapel (and nothing makes me cheerful like going to chapel), I can think calmly, even about the disturbing book of that shrewd writer, Daphne du Maurier, *Vanishing Cornwall*. 'She's one of the best story-tellers in the business', I said to myself. 'But "Vanishing Cornwall?" Not yet. She's out there!'

It may be objected that I have concerned myself with the foothills of chapel life rather than the mountain-top. Of course it was on the mountain-top that the Transfiguration occurred; and also those minor transfigurations known as conversions. But sometimes in these circles one encounters the real thing. To go to Enniscaven ('island or secluded place with elder trees') to visit Alison and Jack Liddicoat was to be aware of this. Mother and father loved to be invited, perhaps for Anniversary. To go through the quiet house to the garden at the back, its rows of potatoes, as is appropriate for early summer earthed up or 'banked' as we say (a job best done with the traditional Cornish shovel) was to partake somewhat of this orderliness of life and spirit. When there, the thought occurred to me more than once: 'John Wesley would have done all right here'. An Anglican clergyman from mid-Cornwall who has spent much of his working life in Leicester, and who is always spoken of by fellow clergy and by lay acquaintance alike in terms of highest praise, owes allegiance to Methodist Enniscaven.

Many in mid-Cornwall will have been saddened, last April, by the news of Alison's death. I recalled that, fifty years ago, she and I both took part in what were called 'sketches', small plays. I remember she played the part of a stupid applicant for a job who had written her own references. 'Oh, I know they're all good,' she said. 'I wrote them myself.' Considering how very intelligent she was, she acted such a part well!

But I am sure Jack will keep that valuable little power-house, Enniscaven Chapel going!

Trezaise congregations were inclined to be timorous and to accept the rule of a father-figure, the tyrannical Cap'n Arthur or the patriarchal Woodman (Woody) Higman. There was a dispute, I have heard, at the opening of Roche cemetery just before the First World War (the old churchyard being full). On each side of a central path there was a considerable portion of burial ground allotted to chapel and to church. For the consecration ceremony the Anglicans had acquired some holy water. The Methodists had none of course; some 'nasty rough Anglicans' put it about that Woody had got hold of a cup from somewhere, and that Woody's Lambs (this was the generic term for Trezaise Methodists) had taken it in turns to piddle in it. The affair came to blows.

I am too young to have known Woody Higman, but I have often heard his son Wilfred preach. Wilfred was a 'long-headed' fellow, assisting in an amateur way in the making of wills, and so on. Wilfred had his head 'to one side', as we say. Uncle Wes (an Anglican) declared it was because his mother had been frightened by a gander when she was 'carryin'' (pregnant). He was a good, but not an emotional preacher. He would have agreed with the preponderance of the rational over the emotional recommended by Jane Austen in one of her letters: 'I am at least persuaded that they who are evangelicals from Reason and Feeling must be happiest and safest'. I have heard father say that one Sunday evening Wilfred Higman brought his sermon to an abrupt halt, with the words: "I'm sorry, brethren. I've lost the thread of my discourse. We'd better have the last hymn, and I'll close the service." A less able man would have struggled on and made the congregation suffer.

I suppose that by every accident of geography and history, and above all by temperament, I align myself with Woody's Lambs. Perhaps the Catholic friends that, greatly daring, I made as an undergraduate at Liverpool University, had the same idea when they gave me the nickname 'Little Bethel'.

I remember one Christmas, a party of Lambs were singing carols for the benefit of a lady universally known as Auntie Fran. She lived near the Rock Hotel; and suddenly a party of very tipsy men came out. They 'glazed' at us, resting their chins on our hymn-books. But, be it stated to the credit of Woody's Lambs, we stood our ground. We had the advantage of being stone-cold sober, whereas they had all the motivation and sense of purpose of bagatelle balls. After a few contemptuous glances, they left.

Like most of Woody's Lambs, I worry too much, and am inclined, in the mid-Cornwall dialect phrase, 'to go Castle (an Dinas) to meet trouble coming from St. Columb.' As one liable to fits of temper and even states of panic, I can choose from a fine array of dialect phrases to describe these: 'bustled up', 'up ninety', 'in some tear', 'vitty hurried', 'properly mazed'. I have also had at least my share of illness. Of all the counsels of courage I have tried, one of the best is a bit of Hebrew bravado. Before a difficult interview, or in a tight spot, I consider the words: 'Though thousands languish and fall beside thee, and tens of thousands around thee perish yet still it shall not come nigh thee. Be not afraid.'

Those words are not in the Authorised Version of the Bible, though the ninety-first Psalm runs them close. The text as I know it is a marriage of two sources, many centuries apart, but both from the same chosen, downtrodden, yet triumphant race. I have not heard these words spoken, but I have heard them sung, and have sung them myself in Trezaise choir. Mr Charlie Trethewey, last and most noted of his generation of Tretheweys, would tap for attention with his baton on the front of the choir, or, as he invariably called it, the orchèstra (correct, if old- fashioned English). He would announce: 'I think for Anniversary evening service we will tackle the Mendelssohn, "Be not afraid", from *Elijah*'.

As I listen again, perhaps to a broadcast, or even in imagination, I recognise the power of these words. Still they speak to the timid, the downcast, the faltering. To Woody's Lambs they speak, diffident, listless, out of kilter. Be not afraid, they say, it is not all bad. There is also hope and renewal. Remember, the stone which the builders rejected, the same is become the head of the corner.

Meanwhile the music (and Trezaise choir in its day was a good sound) reinforces the words at all points. A theme is brewed up by the altos (though thousands languish and fall beside thee), and the sopranos flutter down to receive it (and tens of thousands around thee perish). The tenors, coming in precisely as the baton directs, interweave with the other parts, and the basses bring it all to full fruition.

When my voice broke at the age of about twelve, I was out of the choir for eighteen months; in quarantine, so to speak; redundant, but perhaps with the odd part-time job of picking up the collection. When I went back, I joined the basses; and I understood the phrase 'separating the men from the boys'. As it happened, though there was a varied repertoire, we were re-hearsing the Mendelssohn again. Following the passage I have just described, there is a slow ascending chromatic scale by the basses. It is irresistible, like the bringing up of big guns. All the twiddling and twirling of the higher parts cannot prevail against it.

For a minute or two there is confusion: and so many entries are made that the conductor is hard pressed to introduce them all; his nose twitches slightly, as it is apt to do when he is under stress.

But just when chaos is about to ensue, Mendelssohn, clever man that he is, untangles it all. Tumultuousness subsides. All is unanimous; all is unison, with solid chords of encouragement: 'Be not afraid. I am thy help.'

Woody's Lambs have cheered up. After all, they are Cornish, and most Cornish people love contrapuntal choral music. At the beginning of this book, I mentioned my New Zealand cousin, who gives it on clerical authority that in heaven there will be a great deal of cricket. To quote a dialect phrase, 'I don't go much on that.' But choral music in Heaven is better documented: 'ye choirs of new Jerusalem', for example. I can envisage a very desirable heaven, with perhaps even Felix Mendelssohn Bartholdy, born a Jew but baptised a Christian, conducting; perhaps with Charlie Trethewey as his deputy, tapping with his baton on the orchèstra.

Chapter 6

The Shop

Confusion worse confounded

One wartime Christmas Eve the forecourt of the Phillipps's shop was strewn with hand-made toys, left outside over the dinner- hour. The toys had been made by local carpenters, to substitute for factory-made articles not available 'for the duration'. Father was coming down from Trezaise when a woman stopped him, holding a wooden horse: 'I'll pay for this now, Mr Phillipps,' she said. What she had been trying to do, of course, was steal it. But the remarkable thing was that not more was stolen. Outside the shop was a jumble of galvanised tanks, disconnected lavatory pans, rolls of fencing, barrels of creosote, and cast iron pans for 'coppers' (or furnace pans as they are called in Cornwall). The most ironic thing was that at the corner of the shop window there were two concrete pillars where granda had thoughtfully put them to prevent vehicles damaging the window. But a few years later it was difficult to see the window itself, let alone the pillars, for the many square yards of outdoor stock. Poor granda! The shop was so carefully planned! I once heard him complain, 'I never expected to have to work in muck like this!'

But what about police regulations, by-laws etc? Naturally the situation would not occur today because of more regulations and more dishonesty. The local policeman in the late forties used to grumble occasionally and waxed sarcastic, warning that the outside stock must not go beyond the white line in the middle of the road! However, since the policeman's mother was a tenant in a house of father's he did not proceed very far.

You entered the main shop through a wooden 'hatch' door (double, horizontally divided). The hinges of the lower hatch and the upper hatch were blacksmith made and very heavy. They had need to be, because owing to the piles of ironmongery heaped inside against the door the only way to open it was to unhinge it!

Inside the main shop, like a layer of a more ancient settlement in archaeology, was the blacksmith's forge with an array of tools. The anvil was in the centre, the bellows and cooling trough more to one side. Below the bellows was the coal-pit, dampened in the traditional blacksmith way, by passing water. Through the double doors at the back (though you could rarely get through because of ironmongery) was a yard with a shallow stone trough for 'binding' wooden cart wheels, that is, fitting them with an iron tyre or bind. It was a skilfully planned blacksmith's workshop, built by granda in 1923 or thereabouts; but it is not usual to find bicycles hanging from the roof of a forge, or the floor piled high with oilstoves. There must have been many rows between father and son in the early days; and father told the tale of granda storming down to the ancestral house to grandma: "Come out and look at the mess he got here. Look at it!" Grandma replied: "I ain't goin' look; he's making more money than you ever did." It was true. Brought up on craftsmanship, granda lived to a time when craftsmanship could be seen as self-indulgence.

To move into what we called the little shop, with its separate entrance: directly wall to wall behind the forge in the main shop there was a counter, though it was never used as such because it was piled high with goods and a rather large pair of scales. In the pan of the scales was a big cash-box which was all we had by way of a till. If you think about it, one of those spring tills would have been blocked on the overcrowded counter. The little shop was left empty for quite long periods; and there must, I suppose, have been money taken from the cash-box in the scales from time to time. But not very much, because most Roche people forty or fifty years ago were incorrigibly honest. Some cash fell from the scales to the floor and got lost amid the other detritus. There was a sort of unwritten law that if one of the hangers-on of the shop (there were several of these) found money under the scales it was theirs to keep.

Former customers still occasionally recall to me or to my sister some now distant memories of the shop. One from a Bugle man named Crowle is of going to buy a foster mother. A foster mother is a sort of miniature wooden hut, made of wood but with green baize sides, for day-old chicks to be reared in the warmth of a paraffin heater. Like many items for sale the foster mother, a small one, was dangling from a beam. To get it down necessitated unhooking other articles. Some fell off hooks and the customer caught them. Finally the foster mother fell down and this too was caught by the dexterous Mr Crowle.

"Gravity, Mr Crowle," said my father, "is a wonderful thing!"

Beside the shopkeeping, and running uneasily with it, was the blacksmithing and the farriery. As a qualified farrier, father shoed horses 'routinely' as they say nowadays. Yet to 'put up' four shoes to a horse was half a day's work; and I suppose father still had something of the patrimonial craftsman's instinct, because he would neglect lucrative sales while he dealt with the shoeing of horses. Shoeing a horse entailed preliminary cutting of its toe-nails, so to speak – the ends of the hooves torn off, but painlessly, with the pincers, and filed down with a rasp, or heavy file. The iron shoes, of more or less standard sizes but adjustable on the anvil, were fitted first cold, then hot, with an alarming 'smeech' (a mixture of smoke and stench), and then nailed into place. The special horse-shoe nails were driven through the relatively soft hoof, and 'clinched', or turned over. This was the point of father's shoeing exams; for the hoof and lower foot are obviously vulnerable.

About this word 'clinch': granda did not refer much to the unregenerate Phillippses of former times; but he told me one tale of the Rock Inn, when his ancestor (he did not say which) entered a contest with someone known as The Gipsy King, as to who could tell the biggest lie. The Gipsy King said 'I drove a nail through the moon.' 'I know,' said my ancestor, 'because I was the other side and clinched 'un.'

Many years ago now, I taught a rather artistic student who wore elaborate earrings which I complimented her on. 'You'll never guess what they're made of,' she said, 'they're made of horse shoe nails.'

'They look a bit small to me,' I said. 'I should think they were donkey shoe nails.' 'There now, I didn't know that,' she replied. 'Ah well,' I said, 'a university is a place of learning!'

When shoeing, in a tradition referred to in at least one medieval poem, the blacksmith wore a leather apron, and there was much shouting of 'Giddup' and 'Whey-back' according to whether the horse had to advance or retreat. I think that in the Padstow Hobby Horse cry 'Oss, oss whey oss' the 'whey' is a retreating command. If she could, mother would visit a farmer who was bringing a colt to be shoed, to insist that the animal be tired out before it came to the forge. Father was once in bed for three days after shoeing a restive colt.

Another curious and little-known fact is that blacksmiths usually roll up their sleeves inward, not outward. This is to prevent flying sparks lodging in the rolled sleeves.

When I am tempted to sentimentalise over old 'folkways' and bygone customs, I moderate my nostalgia with the memory of 'binding wheels' in father's blacksmith's shop. How bad-tempered binding wheels made everybody! All the doors would be shut, even on a hot day with both lots of bellows going to keep the rim, covered with ashes, hot all round; then came the quick opening of the doors (the clutter would have to be cleared the day before, probably) and the men would rush out with the white-hot *bind* or 'rim' to the wooden cartwheel waiting on its stone platform. My job was getting buckets of water ready and pouring it as directed: 'Spokehead!' 'Middle of the vally!' – so that the iron tyre or *bind*, suddenly cooled, shrank into the wood. Our dialect *vally* is a quite different word from *valley* spelt with an 'e'. It is a variant of *felloe*, meaning the section of the rim between the spokes.

In all these activities the smith's assistant was the striker; that is, not a militant worker but a man who wields a sledgehammer. My father's striker was called Brice Yeo; and he came from Lerryn on the River Fowey. He had rather a profane tongue. Vexed by circumstances being too uncertain (or as they say nowadays 'iffy') he would say: 'If, if, if, if, if, – if your aunt had balls she'd be your uncle!' Yet, although he would swear 'a hole in an iron pot' as we say, he was really a timid man and also hen-pecked or, as we also say, 'like a toad under a harrow'.

Brice's solace in marital problems, particularly when his wife was what he called 'swaying away', that is nagging, was cigarettes, and Messrs Wills' Woodbines especially. But his wife, Alice, to whom for some reason he gave his father-in-law's name of 'Arry', was accustomed in the dialect phrase to 'lowance him out' with Woodbines. Consequently a brisk trade went on with cigarettes supplied by mother in exchange for eggs that Brice had 'picked up' from his moorland smallholding. Mother often gave him extra Woodbines: 'Cor, missus, you'm a bleddy Christian,' Brice would say; which, apart from the offending epithet, she was. One summer's day, Brice hid one egg in a light jacket he was carrying, and it broke. 'Some order then' as they say in the vernacular. Mother spent a long time washing and drying Brice's jacket, for 'Arry' was a formidable woman. I do not think the crime was ever discovered.

Probably it was his disillusion with marriage that drove Brice to advise my teenage sister frequently: "Don't 'ee get married, chield; stay home with mammy, chield."

Like many other swearers Brice restrained himself in certain company. "What am I supposed to do with this bleddy thing?" he said, gazing at a piece of a plough. Granda, an old-style Methodist who never swore, came up from behind. "I don't see any blood on it, Mr Yeo."

Brice was furious: "You might have told me he was around, Spotty," he said to father. Brice, like many other Cornish people, was a great one for nicknames. Spotty was short for Spotty-belly; a name awarded, I think, with no justification.

I have mentioned the hangers-on of the shop; they were not necessarily young. One in particular was over eighty. He was Mr Jack Harris, awarded because of his assiduous attention to church and especially belfry matters, the title 'Canon' Harris. I remember Canon seated on the forge with granda in the blacksmith's shop, after work had been stopped for the morning or for the day. "Thickey maid, Thomas, where do she come from? She think her piss is champagne don' she?" This might introduce a frequent topic with Canon the Anglican taking the lead; for granda the Methodist had a delicacy in such matters: "I never heard nothing like it," Canon would continue, "Young people these days got to get out two or three times a night to piss. I do sleep all night without getting out once."

A cockney comes to the shop door, playing a mouth-organ: "That's Beethoven's Fifth Symphony, guv'nor," he says to Canon. Canon, even if he mishears, speaks up for the Cornish work-ethic: "You get no sympathy here," he says, "there's plenty of jobs in the claywork and in the quarry. A good day's work is what you need, not sympathy."

Father generally overstocked. Though by nature rather 'near', that is saving, he satisfied the contrary desire, which I suppose we all have at times, to be extravagant, by listening to the wiles (as I felt them to be) of commercial travellers. But one traveller gave offence by advising him not to spend too much: "Thickey fella think I'm goin' scat (bankrupt); I ain't goin' scat. Lot of nonsense!" Another man, a stranger, put his head on the block by quoting the Bible: "This place is overstocked; you must pull down your barns and build greater." He could not be allowed to get away with that: "You go home and read your Bible again, mister. What happens to the man who built bigger barns? God said, "Thou fool. This night thy soul shall be required of thee!"

Father rarely priced new stock and never put it away. Mother and I did that. He would tinker with a few things in the shop, then say, "I'd better see if the churchyard grass is fit to carry". A few shillings' worth of hay given him by the rector was worth more than essential business. Once, in a particularly chaotic situation, mother confided to me: "I sometimes think, Kenneth, that your father is too untidy to be a shopkeeper". I burst out laughing. "You could be right, mother," I said.

However untidy father may have been as a 'stockist', as a salesman he was a joy to listen to: cajoling, teasing, bullying: "Giddaway, you don't want light stone paint. 'Tis a wisht colour that is. No, what you want is blush buff." From which you gather that he was well stocked with blush buff. Or again, "What do 'ee want with one of they short-handled English spades; what you need is a long-handled Cornish shovel. If you ain't careful using they short-handled spades you end up with ducks' disease – backside too near the ground." If a customer was difficult to please, he told them to their face: "You got a fussy customer there, Kenneth."

Mother was an experienced shopkeeper, having worked in a shop for many years; and in token of this she wore a pencil behind her ear. "I had a maid once," said a confirmed bachelor of Roche, "worked in a shop she did. Superior maid she was too. Pencil behind her ear." Mother's line in selling was to appeal, in the case of a young man that she knew was courting, to his sense of gallantry: "How's your heart?" she would ask, having introduced him to a rather expensive article. A rather callow youth seemed to come in from the backwoods every Christmas: "Have 'ee got such a thing as a present for me mam and dad – not too dear?" That settled there would be a pause: "Now, 'ave 'ee got anything for my sweetheart?" "Not too dear?" mother would say provocatively. "Well, I don't mind spending a bit more if 'tis for my sweetheart."

As for my job at Christmas, it was often that of a child-minder; "Kenneth will 'ee take this dear chield into the other shop. I want to pick out his Father Christmas for'n, and I don't want for'n to see."

But the weakness of my position in this matter of the shop was that as a sixth-former and undergraduate I loved the work. I even had a foolish ambition to tidy the shop up, and once I almost did. Things did not last, of course; when I returned to Roche next time there was just as much confusion as before. I reminded myself of the Cornish legend of Tregeagle, draining Dozmary Pool with a leaky limpet shell.

Most customers came to take the untidy shop for granted. It was bound to be untidy with my father in charge. To this day, if you asked anybody over the age of fifty from the china clay area of Cornwall who was the untidiest man they ever knew, they would probably say 'Charlie Phillipps up Roche'. Mr Tarplee, the much-liked rector of the village, knew better than to ask father to look for lost stock. It was true of father, as Hilaire Belloc says of himself: 'A lost thing I could never find, nor a broken thing mend'. 'Kenneth,' Mr Tarplee would say to me, 'can you find a burner corresponding to this lampwick? May I suggest you try the floor?' And as like as not that is where I should find it.

Father countered the suggestion that the shop was full of 'muck' with the Yorkshire proverb: 'Where there's muck there's money'. The losses, naturally, from keeping goods on the ground and in a muddle were very considerable; but he took the view that the real loss to any business was the customer who passed the door without going into the shop. The blacksmithing got more and more crowded out; and I must say I was sorry to see granda almost begging for work till late in his seventies: 'Could 'ee do with a few spikes for these 'ere rabbit-gins, Charlie?' And father would say: 'Better leave'n do it, I suppose, though it do get in the way.'

The variety of our stock delighted father. To a customer asking 'Have 'ee got any oil, Charlie?' he would reply: 'Oil? Hair oil, salad oil, paraffin oil, castor oil, which do you want?' He did not sell salad oil, but he sold two kinds of castor oil, for medicinal or veterinary purposes. Cattle medicine we took well in our stride. It was chiefly supplied by a westcountry firm, Messrs Pinkstone. A smallholder told father, 'If the old cow do cough twice we always give her a drunch of Pinkstone's Curecheline'. In June at the time of the Royal Cornwall Show, the family used to have a free meal in the Pinkstone tent. There were free drinks too, but of course we didn't take those. When I was about twelve I remember a Pinkstone's rep at the Show coming out of the back of the tent and drawing father's attention to the latest kind of antiseptic pessary. Mother said, "Why don't they leave us eat our meal in peace?" But I was very curious. What was a pessary? When next I was in the shop I looked up the veterinary box. A pessary, it said, was a medicated plug, inserted in the cow's vagina after calving, to clean and purify the calf-bag. So that was that!

We sold no food (just as well!) and no clothing except oilers, as we called oilskin jackets and capes, and also oilskin leggings. But we did sell wellington boots and working boots – hob-nailed. I am told farm-labourers often wear trainers now! An occasional problem was that the sizes might get mixed. "I've brought these boots back, Mr Phillipps – they ain't a pair: one seven, one six." Then somebody (but not father) would have the job of re-sorting pairs. Billy Whittam, the boot traveller from Yorkshire, had a habit of calling on Tuesday dinnertimes. Tuesday was pasty day, and father would chop his pasty in two and give Billy half – not so much from generosity as with relief. "You always make such big pasties, mother" he would grumble. But as compensation, for dessert he would have his favourite food: a basin of junket, always eaten with a teaspoon.

How did we come to be selling cough mixture? Goodness knows! Perhaps it was a certain Truro rep for a stationery firm who sold cough mixture on the side – commercial travellers did this sort of thing. The medicine was called White Cross; and its virtues were recommended on the bottle in verse:

> If the chest is tight
> It will put you right.
> It's grateful, comforting
> Gives rest at night.

It would be interesting to know how long White Cross cough mixture has been around. Grateful, in the sense used here, meaning pleasing or gratifying, is hardly twentieth century English; but outstanding poets, of course, do sometimes resort to old-fashioned usage.

But the truth was that White Cross really was efficacious for colds. Once when I had a very heavy cold I took a swig out of one of the bottles, topping it up later with tap water. Since my cold lasted several days I took swigs out of two or three bottles; being careful to choose different ones. After all, our customers were not stupid. I could just imagine the complaints that would be the result of too much dilution: "I'm gone back on that there White Cross trade. First goin' off I thought there was a lot of goodness in it. It done my chest and pipes and that a brave bit of good. But that last bottle I had off you was waiker than teddy-water" (water in which potatoes have been boiled).

Father had an occasional carrier to deliver big articles like galvanised water-tanks, rolls of fencing wire and so on. His name was Mr Dick Allen; and both he and his lorry suited our establishment to a 'T'. The lorry would not possibly pass its MOT test today; but then, father's shop would not help in one of those 'Best-kept village' competitions that are now fashionable! Bits of the lorry kept falling off; but Dick, unperturbed, fixed them on again with his favourite phrase. "We'm all right, ain't us?" he would say as he climbed back into the cab. He was always wonderfully good-tempered. When I was out cycling, on some errand like testing the logan stones on Helman Tor,[1] a loud rattle would herald the approach of our carrier: "Put your bike up over the back, Kenneth". I would do so and climb up with Dick into the front. "We'm brave now, ain't us!"

There was no doubt what came first in our regime. A village fete, an afternoon trip to Newquay (by the Woolworth's train as it was called in the thirties – a cheap excursion) – these were moveable feasts, depending on who was waiting to be served. Father might be cheeky to customers (they liked him for it) but for the rest of us the customer was always right and never to be wrong-footed. When in Roche school we read Cowper's 'John Gilpin', it was not the chase, good though it was, which bore the ring of truth for me; it was the three customers who delayed the start of the excursion;

> For saddle-tree scarce reached had he
> His journey to begin,
> When, turning round his head he saw
> Three customers come in.
>
> So down he came; for loss of time
> Although it grieved him sore,
> Yet loss of pence, full well he knew,
> Would trouble him much more.

If, which I am reluctant to admit, those men who were the elders of my youth had a fault, it was parsimoniousness, a tendency to be 'near', as we called it. This could make shopkeeping difficult. A customer would say, 'I want half a pound of wire nails – more four inch than three inch, more three inch than two inch.' You only get about eight nails for half a pound in any case! Nails were sixpence (old pence) a pound; so half a pound necessitated parting with a twelve-sided threepenny bit, tipped out carefully into the rim of a leather purse lid, and handed over as if it were a portion of the crown jewels.

Most springs a series of rather sad orders, father thought, came from Trezaise from half a dozen house-proud couples wanting paint and decorating materials. These men, old by the nineteen-

[1] My friend Bryn Lean solemnly warned me once: "If you'm doing this sort of thing now, Charlie, what will you be like by the time you'm sixty?"

fifties, had built their own houses 'out of coor' (in their spare time) in some cases in what they had regarded as a golden age, the Liberal Government of 1906–1916. With all that concentration on architecture they were childless. The white paint and coloured distemper they bought from Phillipps' shop were no substitute.

A sore point in the shop concerned the selling of creosote. There is no more pernicious commodity to stock and sell; it permeates irredeemably, and stinks to high heaven. I ruined a pair of trousers hopelessly stained; mother several pairs of stockings. The stuff was sold from a metal barrel, kept out of doors of course so that anybody could have helped themselves in any case! The barrel had a pump which 'skit', that is leaked and splashed. It amused me to find, in Dr A.L.Rowse's *A Cornish Childhood*, the author complaining at having to sell lamp-oil in the family shop. One might compare the Old Testament threats of Rehoboam about chastising with whips and scorpions: 'My father also chastised you with lamp-oil, but I will chastise you with creosote'.

Eventually we sold creosote separately packaged in cans. Then, naturally, there was 'some order', as we say, meaning contradictorily 'some disorder, some chaos'; with a great deal of protest: "'Tis heaps cheaper when 'tis sold loose". 'Loose creosote' is a bit like that now fashionable phrase, 'a loose cannon'.

Only slightly less evil-smelling than creosote was something we called *carbine*. A carbine in standard English is a kind of gun; but when customers asked for a tin of 'carbine' they brought a Tate and Lyle two-pound treacle tin. Where the weights and measures people came in I do not know. *Carbine* was in fact calcium carbide, kept in a big drum and sold in the form of what looked like small stones. A treacle-tin-full cost a shilling. The stuff was put in the front light of a cycle and it gave out acetylene gas when a trickle of water was poured on it, and this burnt with a bright light. When I was little a customer said to me, "Do you want to see water burn?" There was a pigs' trough outside the shop filled with rainwater; sure enough, when he put a match to it a flame appeared in the water.

It will come as no surprise that our accounts as well as our stock were often in a muddle. One of the chief reasons for this was miserliness. Father saved nothing more keenly than paper, and instead of methodically recording the day's items and takings in a day-book, for later ledger entry, he would insert the odd scrap of an entry in a gap to save paper. I suggested to him more than once that we could not afford his economies. One of my abiding memories of mid-Cornwall, and one that informs my belief that the working-class people of the mid-Cornwall of my youth were the salt of the earth, was the constant cry of the customers: "When can we have our bill, Mr Phillipps?" "Oh, well" father would say, "the boy's home for a week or two now; we'll get some of them out". I'm afraid, what with one thing and another, the accounts, like bookkeeping in H.G.Wells's *History of Mr Polly*, 'were pursued but never effectively overtaken'. There must have been a great many unpaid bills when father died. The truth was that the shop had become bigger than the staff who ran it. When I saw the cartoon version of 'The Sorcerer's Apprentice' (Walt Disney) in *Fantasia* I felt there was a striking similarity with our shop; and there was no controlling magician to set things right in the end.

Of course, there were longstanding debts. We had labels to stick on bills to threaten debtors with. The last and fiercest was a scarlet one: 'Unless a remittance is forwarded within seven days proceedings will be taken'. If the erring customer would believe this he would believe anything. For nobody was ever proceeded against.

But father didn't always lose by being too trusting, and by heeding the dictum: 'The confidence trick is the work of man, but the want-of-confidence-trick is the work of the devil'. A bankrupt man said to him: "Charlie, if you don't send in my account to the receiver in the bankruptcy court I'll pay you up, every bleddy penny". Father did not send in the account and in time the bankrupt paid him up, 'every bleddy penny'.

Our prices were, as they say, fairly competitive, and we gave generous discounts for ready money. It is curious that the price of one item of stock remains in my head: thus throughout most of the war years a new bicycle cost, as father put it, 'sixpence short of nine pounds'. (Incidentally, the handle-bars in war-time were not chromium plated but black japanned). Father would add, 'but eight pounds ten will pay it' – that was his formula. You could pay it all by instalments, for which we supplied little notebooks. Since the customers were often no more systematic than the shopkeeper, from time to time these books were lost. "What be us goin' do by you? Ought to have your ass kicked, losing your payin'-in book!"

Out of curiosity when in Leicester recently I walked into a large cycle shop, Julie's. Julie started several years ago as a teenager, and the business is now of a kind to warm the cockles of that conjectural organ, Margaret Thatcher's heart. I enquired the price of a single-speed, sit-up-and-beg bicycle. The bike that had been 'sixpence short of nine pounds' was now £159. But of course, this being Leicester, the shopkeeper said "You're looking at a hundred and sixty pounds". As to extra gears, "You get what you pay for!"

Despite his sister's jibe that he was 'cheating the public', father did not, on the whole, cheat, except under provocation. I remember once he was trying to sell a handbrush to a difficult customer, who asked, 'You haven't got one of a rather better quality, Mr Phillipps?'

Father went to the back of the shop, and produced the same brush, except for a different coloured back "This one is a bit stiffer in the bristle, I think you will find," he said, increasing the price.

When the lady left with her brush, I gave the shopkeeper a quizzical look. 'Well, everybody's happy, aren't they?' he said.

The fact that he overstocked, and traded with a number of firms, worked out to his advantage in wartime. A large number of household items were scarce: vacuum flasks, primus stove burners, tins of stove polish (they would hardly be needed now), cups with handles. A pair of customers once said to him, 'We've tried all over the place, Mr Phillipps, but we said to ourselves, we're bound to get it here.' You should have tried here first,' father would reply. 'We've just sold the last one!' There was no doubt that he enjoyed 'aggravating'. Mother would remind him. 'oil is cheaper than sandpaper'.

A manciple (it is Chaucer's word, but it ought to be still in use, and probably still is in ancient universities) – a manciple, or an officer who purchases provisions for an institution, used to come from the County mental hospital in Bodmin, taking away carloads of goods. His name was Peter Sandry. 'I suppose you think,' he said, 'that we shan't come near this place after the war when things are plentiful. Well, you are quite right; we shan't.'

When father was thinking of retiring and selling the business, he received what would be considered an accolade in the south-west: a customer wrote to what was then Westward, the Plymouth ITV centre: there was a well-known 'character' they should interview. David Mudd, then a television journalist, later a Cornish M.P., came down with cameras.

Mother was most scornful of the process. 'Father had to come round the corner and meet David Mudd as a surprise. Three times they practised that surprise!' I did not see the programme, but in middle-class company, father's style was apt to be a little cramped. Still, they would have filmed the mountains of 'stuff', as we called it. It is a dubious honour that, as a family, we owned the most untidy shop in Cornwall. Certainly, its like will not be seen again.

One evening in September, 1992, I went to Withiel, the village adjoining Roche to the north, to give a talk on dialect. It had been raining but cleared to a perfect evening. Withiel, with its patchwork of fields, especially after harvest, is more beautiful than the more industrial Roche. My New Zealand cousin suggested to me that heaven will be like a cricket match. I doubt this; but if heaven is like Withiel, as perhaps it may be, I shall not complain. However, I suppose that people, not used to country life, could not live there; no shops, no pub; only the pinnacled church and the brand new village hall.

It was there that I gave the talk; the questions such as arose were answered. Then followed refreshments; provided by the W.I. and therefore good.

I was sitting on the platform, eating, when a procession of people came up, not with questions, but with anecdotes about my father – most of the farmers hereabouts had been his customers. Usually the subject was his special kind of cheek: 'Do you know what your father said to me? I complained that some of the nails he was selling were rusty! He said, "We don't charge no more for the rust."' 'A visitor to Roche asked your father, "Do you know all that you got here, Mr Phillipps?" He said, "Not right now, because I don't know who you are; but I mostly know what's here."' Somebody remembered that she had made a mistake in an order for father: "You go back home" he said, "and tell 'em to send back somebody that know something about it."'

There were many more such tales, still remembered though father had been dead eleven years. Some little Withiel concerns, like Mr Thorn Hawken's 'shoemakerin' business, were serviced from the shop. I was very impressed at my father's funeral to find a packed chapel, and practically all his regular customers from the hinterland attending.

The secret, I suppose, was personality. This is why many liked him, and a few hated him. Most of 'we Phillippses', it must be confessed, have to stand up twice to make a shadow. Except in old age, father was mostly flamboyant; perhaps he 'turned after' the Knights. But the quotation that I most often recall when thinking of him is from a masterly short story in our dialect by Anne Treneer, 'Old Mr Trebilcock'. As I contrast my father and me Anne Treneer's words still strike home: 'Had his own way when he was young, and had his own way when he was old . . . not like some poor toads that can't call their toenails their own, leave alone their souls.'

I recall him now, quickly unrolling and measuring some wire-netting down the lane by the shop. You had to be quick because vans and tractors could come up the lane the other way. But he would go dancing along, his metal two-foot rule in his hand. Since there was no counter the customers came down the lane, their money in their fists. There would be an exchange of sarcasm, and the job would be done.

He himself summed up his philosophy very succinctly: "I don't go much on these here pop songs," he said to me, "but there's one song I *do* like – the one that Frank Sinatra do sing: 'I did it my way.' "